STAR TREK

Borgo Press Books by Michael Hemmingson

The Rose of Heaven
In the Background Is a Walled City
How to Have an Affair and Other Instructions
Auto/Ethnographies: Sex, Death, and Symbolic Interaction
The Stripper: A Tale of Lust and Crime
The Dirty Realism Duo: Charles Bukowski and Raymond Carver
Sexy Strumpets and Troublesome Trollops
Seven Women: An Erotic Private Investigation
Judas Payne
Star Trek: A Post-Structural Critique
Zona Norte

FOR OTHER PRESSES

The Naughty Yard (Permeable Press, 1994)
Crack Hotel (Permeable Press, 1995)
Minstrels (Permeable Press, 1997)
The Mammoth Book of Short Erotic Novels (Carroll & Graf, 2000)
The Mammoth Book of Legal Thrillers (Carroll & Graf, 2001)
Wild Turkey (Forge, 2001)
The Comfort of Women (Blue Moon, 2002)
The Dress (Blue Moon, 2002)
My Fling with Betty Page (Eraserhead Press, 2003)
Drama (Blue Moon, 2003)
The Rooms (Blue Moon, 2003)
The Lawyer (Blue Moon, 2003)
House of Dreams Trilogy (Avalon, 2004)
The Garden of Love (Blue Moon, 2004)
Expelled from Eden: A William T. Vollmann Reader (Thunder's
    Mouth Press, 2004)
This Other Eden (The Dybbuk Press, 2009)
Amateurs (Olympia Press, 2009)
William T. Vollmann: A Critical Study (McFarland, 2009)
William T. Vollmann: An Annotated Bibliography (Scarecrow Press,
    2010)
Gordon Lish and His Influence on 20th Century American Literature
    (Routledge, 2010).
The Reflexive Gaze of Critifiction (Guide Dog Books, 2010)
Women in the Short Stories of Raymond Carver (McFarland, 2010)

STAR TREK

A Post-Structural Critique
of the Original Series

by

Michael Hemmingson

The Borgo Press

An Imprint of Wildside Press LLC

MMIX

CONTENTS

DEDICATION

TO MY PARENTS

and

FOR LIV KELLGREN

*"Her life could have been as rich as any woman's,
if only... if only..."*

—Captain James T. Kirk, "Turnabout Intruder"

For the last ten or fifteen years, the immense and proliferating criticizability of things, institutions, practices, and discourses; a sort of general feeling that the ground was crumbling beneath our feet, especially in places where it seemed most familiar, most solid, and closest to us, to our bodies, to our everyday gestures. But alongside this crumbling and the astonishing efficacy of discontinuous, particular, and local critiques, the facts were also revealing something […] beneath this whole thematic, through it and even within it, we have seen what might be called the insurrection of subjugated knowledges.

—MICHEL FOUCAULT, *SOCIETY MUST BE DEFENDED*

To each his own bauble.

—JEAN BAUDRILLARD, *THE ECSTASY OF COMMUNICATION*

"Are you out of your Vulcan mind?!"

—DR. MCCOY TO MR. SPOCK

TEASER

Postmodern Wagon Train to the Stars

NBC first aired *Star Trek* on September 8, 1966, with "The Man Trap." The starship *Enterprise*'s plucky, low-budget crew visits the planet M-113 on a routine check-up. Dr. Carter and his wife Nancy, a former paramour of Dr. McCoy's, are studying the remains of an ancient civilization on what they believe is an unoccupied world. A member of the landing party is killed (the disposable extra landing party character, often referred to as a "red shirt"), his body drained of salt, peculiar marks left on his face. While this was the first *aired* episode, it is the sixth storyline in the original line-up, with a Stardate of 1513.1 (the chronology of ship time while in space).[1] The tenth episode to air, "The Corbomite Maneuver" (11/10/66) is chronologically set Stardate 1512.2, whereas the sixth, "Mudd's Women" (10/13/66) precedes at Stardate 1329.8.[2] This lack of a broadcasted linear timeline had to do with postproduction progress per episode; scripts needing less special effects were aired when ready.

I was two months old on that original airdate. I did not catch it the first time out. I did not start watching the series until I was seven or eight, long after its cancellation. *Star Trek* had three seasons and plenty of history by then; to me it was new, just like reruns of other science-fictional shows *My Favorite Martian*, *Land of the Giants*, *UFO*, *Voyage to the Bottom of the Sea*, and *Time Tunnel* were "new" to children of my generation during syndication. I was not seriously interested in science-fiction until *Star Wars* (1977), when *Star Trek* was immensely popular in re-runs across the globe. The success of *Star Wars* generated a new set of fans—and rekindled interest from old fans—in entertainment set in the future, another galaxy, and among the stars. Series such as the original *Battlestar Galactica* and *Buck Rogers in the 25th Century* also found an audience among these post-*Star Wars* fans.

Why did *Star Trek* have a tough time staying on the air in the late 1960s, was cancelled and revived, and the *Enterprise*'s five-year mission cut short? There have been a number of explanations: a corporate bias against science-fiction, a negative reaction by the network toward the multi-cultural cast and the "utopian" view of the future ("utopia" in quotes will become apparent later), the network continuously changing the date and times when the show aired, so viewers did not know when the next episode would air. Despite these challenges, *Star Trek*'s post-broadcast life has been an anomaly of the business and a phenomenon of television history.

Looking back, there is much to find amusing and even ridiculous: cheap alien costumes with visible seams; the *Enterprise* model dangling on strings or moving through "space" in a jagged, awkward manner; Styrofoam and plywood sets; melodramatic and over-the-top acting; absurd storylines (entire planetary civilizations resembling Chicago in the 1920s, Nazi Germany, or ancient Rome); repetitive themes (humans being tested by superior alien races); questionable science and technology.[3] These attributes must be taken into context, however: perhaps "silly" today, when compared to the evolution of television content and special effects, but progressive in the late 1960s when science-fiction was still relatively new territory and the popular dramatic programming were westerns and courtroom dramas.

Star Trek fans ("Trekkies" or "Trekkers") can watch episodes of what is referred to as "TOS" (The Old or Original Series) over and over; they know the plots inside-out, can recite monologues, soliloquies, and dialogue verbatim; they find wisdom in the self-righteous, bombastic pontifications of Captain Kirk when he either wax philosophizes about human nature, peaceful exploration, and freedom, or tricks a robotic machine with fuzzy logic and reasoning, coupled with actor William Shatner's trademark verbal inflections, hand gestures, and facial expressions that have now become an institution for the actor and iconic for the series. The viewer knows all is in good hands when it comes to the hegemony and agency of Kirk, because he will save the ship and save the day—the Galaxy![4]—and off they go on the next adventure.

* * * * * * *

This monograph is an examination of the original series (herein "TOS") only, with the occasional sidebar on the animated series, feature films, the four off-shoot series, and related original novels. Within the context of television studies, my argument consists of two parts:

(1) No other show in the history of broadcast television has affected and influenced society, science, language, psychology, fan culture and consumerism (combined, "the real world") the way *Star Trek* has. The show is an example of Jean Baudrillard's theories of hyperreality and simulacra—*Star Trek* is a fiction that shapes reality outside the television screen; its signs and images penetrate the culture that created it, infiltrate psyches and living rooms; implants itself inside and outside the mind and re-shapes that world; by way of cultural mimesis, *Star Trek* acquires new fans every generation who are often the off-spring, siblings, nephews, nieces, and cousins of older fans who tune into re-runs or play old episodes on DVD, indoctrinating these new viewers. Next to *Star Wars* and *The Lord of the Rings* (2001-03) trilogy, no other fictional entertainment is imitated, through acts of hyper-reality, by hundreds of thousands of fans, encompassing clothing,

philosophy, personal and spiritual beliefs, communicative gestures, and ideology.

(2) Although *Star Trek* is set in an alleged galactic utopian society led by human beings, with earth as home base for the Federation, the storylines, and general atmosphere of the universe the characters live in, do not always resemble the concepts of the typical utopia where equality, peace, and freedom of choice reign. The Federation and its military arm, Starfleet, are not as pious as its PR machine would like aliens across the galaxy to believe. The *Enterprise* is an armed warship; Captain Kirk and crew kill alien life and others humans alike when it suits their purpose. The Federation has an imperialist philosophy within its ambitious expansion and colonization efforts, spreading the English language and human morals across the solar systems, often forcing a narrow ideology on other cultures. The first rule the Starfleet officers supposedly live by is a non-interference mandate, the "Prime Directive," yet we see the rules of the Prime Directive continuously violated as societies of the Other are infiltrated and forced to accept Federation dogma and human (American) notions of democracy and freedom.

* * * * * * *

I call this a post-structural critique because I reject older views of television criticism that purports to hold an "absolute truth" in the critical methods and theory when approaching televisual texts. Just as the structure of a series episode in the 1960s is quite different than one in the twenty-first century, so must be the critic's gaze of television's past. Media studies in television suffer today from almost modernist methods with both the visual text and the written text that critiques it. Post-structuralism rejects the idea of any text having a single purpose, a single meaning, or one singular existence; the single reader creates a new and individual purpose, meaning, and existence for a given text. We shall see this is true for the *Star Trek* fans that have created a reality where the imaginary *Star Trek* universe has more meaning than the physical universe they live in.

* * * * * * *

The structure of this monograph represents the breakdown of a one-hour teleplay: a teaser, four acts, and a coda (or credit window), with endnotes between acts as commercial breaks. We can say *it has a structure.*

In Act I, I consider the politics of broadcast entertainment, and what series creators must go through to put their dreams on the boob tube. In Act II, I discuss the political, social, and cultural climate of the United States in the late 1960s, and how the atmosphere of the times influenced storylines of *Star Trek.* In Act III, I show how a teleplay evolves from idea to script to episode with "The City on the Edge of Forever" (4/6/67), arguably one of the most popular episodes of the series. In Act IV, I examine various episodes that support the second point of my thesis, and represent the political agenda, foreign policy, and positions on war within the Federation's hegemonic presence across the galaxy that do not quell with utopian thought. I also summarize how *Star Trek* has evolved beyond the first three seasons and become a profitable franchise for Paramount Studios and CBS, encompassing five spin-off series, books, audio tapes, video games, eleven feature films, various merchandise, and fan fiction, written or filmed.

It is my intent for the reader to view *Star Trek* in a different critical context than what has already been written regarding gender, fandom, and the post-human in science-fiction television studies. I contend that the *Enterprise*'s mission and the policies of Starfleet do more harm than good to other races and cultures, which of course reflects the political beliefs of the United States involvement in Vietnam and desire to spread the virtues of capitalism and the American version of democracy. Despite the message creator Gene Roddenberry intended at the start, there are a number of forces, inside and outside the network offices, which influence a television show to stray from its ideological path: crises in society, pressure by advertisers, biases of executives who make final decisions, and the network Office of Standards and Practices. What we see on our television sets, the content we absorb, has taken a long road to get there, with many minds involved, each with an agenda and vision of what a show will represent and what ideas and concepts are, at the moment of broadcast, socially and culturally acceptable.

Commercial Break: Notes

1. The *Star Trek* website memory-alpha.org explains the Stardate system has "little relationship to Earth's time as we know it; one hour aboard a starship at different impulse speeds may equal many Earth hours. Stardates are calculated through a complicated equation that takes into account relativistic effects, universal expansion and the effects of gravity on time and space. Every so often the stardate system has to be updated to take into account the expansion of space or other natural effects." In *The Making of Star Trek*, Gene Roddenberry states that stardates were created to avoid placing the events of the original series within a specific A.D. year. For detailed information on the Stardate system, see http://memory-alpha.org/en/wiki/Stardate.

2. One of the animated episodes, "The Magicks of Megas-Tu" (10/27/73) is set Stardate 1254.4, the only animated episode taking place before the events of *Star Trek*'s first season.

3. David Gerrold, in *The Trouble with Tribbles* (1973) admits he had a problem with the science of the transporter when he watched the first episodes. He felt the "technology" made no sense because there would need to be a "receiving" station on the other end where they could transport to, and transport back. Teleportation was Roddenberry's answer to budget con-

straints—it would be too expensive to have the *Enterprise* land on and depart planet surfaces.

4. There are minor flaws of consistency. Lieutenant Uhura wears a tan uniform in "The Corbomite Maneuver" and a red one, which she dons throughout the rest of the series, in "The Man Trap." Why the uniform and rank change, when tan denotes a higher officer's position than red?

ACT I

"LET'S GET THE HELL OUT OF HERE": THE POLITICS OF BROADCAST TELEVISION

PLAYING THE HOLLYWOOD GAME

In his introduction to "The City on the Edge of Forever," from the anthology *Six Science Fiction Plays* (1973), Harlan Ellison writes:

> Gene Roddenberry called me to say he had sold a series to NBC called "Star Trek." "It's going to be a sophisticated 'Wagon Train to the Stars,'" Gene said; and we both laughed. We laughed, because Gene was making fun of the tunnel-vision thinking of many television network programming clowns who cannot perceive any new property in an original way. (5)

The Western had been a popular format in the 1950s-1960s, so it was "just another horse opera except they ride a spaceship instead of a nag" (*The Making of Star Trek* 22). Roddenberry also pitched *Star Trek* as "Horatio Hornblower in space." Like a wagon train making its way across the American desert, seeking a place to call home, it was a bumpy and uncertain road to get *Star Trek* on the air and keep it there. Roddenberry had to dodge numerous obstacles and jump through a variety of hoops; this is true for any series creator—the politics of television culture and the business of broadcasting are tricky waters to navigate and requires a great deal of compromise, game playing, questionable ethics, smooth-talking, back-patting (or stabbing) and empirical ass-kissing. It takes a certain "kind" of person to survive in television production, proving that one has "what it takes" to deal with the hardships, negativity, and uncertainty that is endemic of the community. What is embraced one day is reviled the next; one can be told "yes" on Monday and "no" on Friday by the same entities, and vice versa, without explanation. Roddenberry proved he was made for the television game; he had a burning desire to succeed and would not take "no" for an answer; he was a former World War II bomber pilot, and had a go-getter, fighting attitude necessary for a career in television.

Having published stories in the pulp magazines and believing he had "the right stuff" for Hollywood, Roddenberry moved to Los Angeles to find work as a writer, taking a job with the Los Angeles Police Department to pay the bills. He had to write scripts under a pen name because the LAPD did not approve of employees moonlighting; when he started earning four times the amount of money he was making as a police sergeant, he quit the force. That job inspired the creation of *The Lieutenant*, a cop show that lived for one season, and put Roddenberry in the right position to present and pitch his ideas for new shows. While he enjoyed writing for others, he understood that to make a significant salary, and to hold a power position in the industry, creating and producing his own series was more lucrative and satisfying than wearing the writer's hat in someone else's playground. Most episodes for programs were written by freelancers, not a full-time writing staff as is the norm today, so not having one's own show subjected a writer to unsteady paychecks. Roddenberry eventually secured a three-year development deal with Desilu Productions, owned by Desi Arnaz and Lucille Ball.

Star Trek was first offered to CBS, which turned it down in favor of *Lost in Space* (1965-68). When *Star Trek* was cancelled after its second season, fifty-four episodes in the vault, Roddenberry knew that there would be no syndication life without at least a third season. *Star Trek* could have easily vanished the way many programs that last one or two seasons do—networks have vast libraries of shows that have come and gone out of the cultural meme; a few, such as *Wonderfalls* (2004, Fox) with only fourteen episodes, still survive with niche fans, cable syndication, and strong foreign rights. Roddenberry encouraged fans to write letters to NBC, demanding the show stay on air. The letter campaign worked, now part of the *Star Trek* mythos[1] —*Star Trek* returned for one more season, but "they found it was a pyrrhic victory," claims Kate Helman in her review of the Season Three DVD box set, noting Roddenberry became less involved as

> NBC moved *Star Trek* from its coveted slot of 8:00 PM on Monday night to the deadly 10:00 PM Friday night schedule. This meant a significant audience loss from *Star Trek*'s younger demographic, and was a clear sign that NBC had very little interest in a season four [....] Not surprisingly, with increasingly smaller budgets [...] and a shrinking audience, the third season is the most uneven and weakest year in the life of the series. (n.p.)

There was no clean wrap-up. *Star Trek* ended on an anti-climatic episode with "Turnabout Intruder" without any indication the show had come to a close.

ACTORS

William Shatner was a trained Shakespearian actor who had been working on the theater stages in Canada since he was a child. He made his screen debut as Alexi in *The Brother Karamazov* (1958), alongside Yul Brynner. On television, he had guest roles on *The Big Valley, The Fugitive, The Man from U.N.CL.E., Alfred Hitchcock Pre-*

sents, *The Virginian*, *The Outer Limits*, and forgotten shows such as *77 Sunset Strip*, *The Nurses*, and *Outlaws*. His best known pre-*Star Trek* role is an episode from *The Twilight Zone*, "Nightmare at 20,000 Feet" (11/11/ 63), playing a paranoid man on an airplane that keeps seeing a "gremlin" on the wing (a man in a big fuzzy pajama suit), dismantling the plane's electric wiring. He was cast in a courtroom drama, *For the People* (1963), cancelled after thirteen episodes, unable to compete in the same timeslot as *Bonanza* (1959-73, NBC). When he was offered *Star Trek*, he finally had a regular paycheck to play the Iowa farm boy who dreamed of the stars and excelled in the military to become, at age thirty-five, Starfleet's youngest captain.

Leonard Nimoy, DeForest Kelley, and James Doohan were character actors making a meager living in Hollywood. The multi-racial cast on the bridge was a first for broadcast TV, showing minorities in positions of authority, especially an Asian and an African-American. (In Shatner's 2006 *Comedy Central* roast, he says jokingly, "We had an Asian driver and a black woman in front of a screen who wasn't yelling at it.") George Takei's Mr. Sulu did not receive a first name, Hikaru, until 1981 in Vonda N. McIntyre's novel, *The Entropy Effect*; the name did not become canon until used in the feature film *Star Trek VI: The Undiscovered Country* (1991). Throughout TOS, he was provided little background history, but over the course of various episodes, bits of biographical and personal information were revealed. Sulu is a San Francisco native; in *Star Trek IV: The Voyage Home* (1986), he gazes on the city as it was in the 1980s (after traveling back in time) and says, proudly, "I was born there." His original position on the *Enterprise* was astrophysicist; he was quickly promoted to helmsman on the bridge, where he remained until becoming a captain himself and given the *U.S.S. Excelsior* to command. He was the only consistent officer at helm control; the show went through a number of navigators, until finally settling on Ensign Chekov in the second and third seasons.

Takei "came out" as a homosexual in 2005; this was official but those who knew him in Los Angeles knew his sexual orientation. It was news to fans, however; for many years, gay, lesbian, and transgender fans waited, and lobbied, for the day a homosexual character would appear in one of the series or films. This never happened until the 1990s in the novels, and with resistance from the franchise. Roddenberry was accused of being homophobic: in his utopia there was no place for gay men and women in Starfleet, albeit all the inter-species relations going on. James Satter, in his essay "The Hidden Homosexual," claims Sulu to be "distinctly symbolic of a closeted gay man" (*Science Fiction Studies* 380). Since Takei's disclosure, *Star Trek* fans and scholars have new context to interpret Sulu, looking for clues of the queer in his character—such as the fact he never has a romantic storyline with a woman while every other male character does; his heavy application of make-up and eyeliner (yet other male actors seemed to do this as well); and although he exhibits masculinity, there are other times he has effeminate traits. There is also his polar opposite in the alternate universe episode "Mirror, Mirror" (10/6/67), where he is portrayed as a chauvinistic, womanizing skirt-chaser. If everyone's double is the exact opposite in this universe, the proof was there—he had to be gay in the *Star Trek* universe. Satter refers to this as "the gay lens" (381) on Sulu—the implication that Takei was subtle in hinting at Sulu's truth.

Martin Luther King recognized the importance of *Star Trek*'s multi-racial casting. In her memoir, *Beyond Uhura* (1994), Nichelle Nichols recounts how, after the first season came to a close, she informed Roddenberry that she wanted to leave the show and go back to theater. She was introduced to Reverend Martin Luther King, Jr., at an NAACP event and King spoke of the importance of her character as an African-American woman in a high-ranking position and what that meant to the African-American community; he told her Uhura's presence was changing the face of television. Dr. King also convinced Nichols to stay on the show. Getting her originally cast was another matter; Roddenberry fought hard to hire her, despite network disapproval, and Nichols admits, in her memoir, that Roddenberry's actions were proprietary: she had a short romantic fling with him, apparently at the same time he was involved with Majel Barrett (Nurse Chapel), whom he eventually married.

Leonard Nimoy was not comfortable with the off-screen association as a logical green-blooded half-human. When the re-runs became popular, he wrote *I Am Not Spock* (1976) to distance himself from the alien he portrayed; twenty years later, however, he wrote a second memoir, *I Am Spock* (1995) embracing his alter-ego. In the beginning, NBC executives rejected Spock's appearance: the pointed ears and upturned eyebrows, they felt, looked "satanic" and they worried viewers would find this unsavory and upsetting; these features were airbrushed out of promotional materials send out to network affiliates. This look, as Nimoy points out in *I Am Spock*, became a "sex symbol" (85) to female fans. Although he has a strong television résumé prior to *Star Trek*, Nimoy's attempts at an acting career after the series did not bode well in the mainstream, just as Shatner appeared in a series of low-budget, B-grade horror movies, and the soft-X *Big Bad Mama* (1974) with Angie Dickinson. Nimoy won acclaim for many stage and guest television roles. His appearance in the second re-make of *Invasion of the Body Snatchers* (1978), co-starring with Donald Sutherland, and his narration of the documentary show, *In Search Of...* (1976-82, NBC), proved that the public responded well to Nimoy within the genre of the fantastic.

DeForest Kelley, who played Dr. Leonard "Bones" McCoy, appeared in two 1967 pilots helmed by Gee Roddenberry, *33 Montgomery* and *Police Story* that were not picked up. He made his screen debut in *Fear in the Night*

(1947), a low budget crime story that was unexpectedly successful. He often portrayed villains in *Perry Mason*, *Gunsmoke*, *Bonanza*, and other shows, and feared he would be typecast, which happened after *Star Trek*—except for a small re-occurring role in *Ironside*, Kelley experienced difficulty finding work until McCoy was revived for the feature films. He died in 1999 of stomach cancer, his ashes scattered over the Pacific Ocean.

When James Doohan died in 2005, NASA launched his ashes into Earth's orbit on a Falcon One rocket, along with astronaut Gordon Cooper's ashes, a member of Project Mercury that sent the first Americans into space. This was NASA's nod to Chief Engineer Montgomery Scott's (Scotty) influence. Without Scotty, the *Enterprise* would have broken down in space many times, missions would have failed, and landing parties would have not been able to beam back up.

TV "FIRSTS"

Two "firsts" in television history occurred on *Star Trek*: the first time the word "hell" (or any swear word) was spoken on air in "The City on the Edge of Forever" (4/6/67), and the first broadcast interracial kiss, between Kirk and Lieutenant Uhura, in "Plato's Stepchildren" (11/22/68).[2] At the end of "City," Kirk, having lost the love of his life to save the universe, says, "Let's get the hell out of here." It was a "shocking" moment in television, and resulted in a number of angry letters from the offended and provincial. In "Plato's Stepchildren," a megalomaniac tyrant uses his power of mind over matter and forces Kirk and Uhura into an embrace and kiss. The two are unable to fight it; the kiss is strained, hardly romantic or sexual, and they do not "lock lips." Kirk apologizes and Uhura admits that in the past, during crises situations when the ship and crew were in danger, she always felt safe seeing him in the captain's chair, knowing he would them through safely. This indicates that the kiss is not so bad for her and all along she has been harboring an attraction to her boss. Public reaction to the kiss was both vitriolic for its crossing racial boundaries and commendable for its progressive representation of breaking down the racial boundaries.

VISUALS

Star Trek was shot in bright Technicolor® which enhanced the blue, red, and gold tunics worn by the characters, and the soft pastel hues of the ship walls, all on low-budget, limited sets. Most exterior scenes on alien planets were done on sound stages, often with the same plastic rocks and empty, background sky, with a color change. A few episodes were shot at outdoors locations, such as "Arena" (1/16/67), where Kirk battles the Gorn captain at

Vasquez Rocks, north of Los Angeles County.[3] Faster-than-light warp drive depicted the stars of the Galaxy trailing by as if gazing through a convex lens, an image that is both iconic and a motif of the show, regardless of his fuzzy science. Art director Matt Jeffries was a former World War II airman and designed the interiors of the *Enterprise*—the bridge and crew quarters—in what he felt space traveling humans would find comfortable and ergonomic. The bridge is spacious, a flutter with blinking lights and melodious computer sounds. The uniforms were simple, snug, and for women (as discussed later), revealing. The automatic doors that opened to the ship's turbolift were a novel visual and convenient concept, later incorporated by architects. Stock footage, re-used sets, less outdoors settings, and less outer space action in the third season were due to severe budget cuts. By then, "top writers, top guest stars, top anything you needed was harder to come by," notes Nichelle Nichols (*Beyond Uhura* 189).

SOUND

Alexander Courage wrote the theme score, played over both the opening and closing credits of the original series. The opening credits begin with William Shatner's monologue: "Space: the final frontier...," and the theme begins, interspersed with the *Enterprise* flying toward and past the camera with a dramatic "whoosh"[4] as if the ship were racing toward its next great adventure. The theme song is reprised over the closing credits, overlaying stills from various episodes. Unknown to Courage at the time, Roddenberry wrote lyrics to the theme, not to be sung but to claim fifty percent of the performance royalties. Courage did not engage in litigation over the matter and later publicly stated he felt this was unethical of Roddenberry; this also caused Courage to walk away from the show. With the budget tightening, *Star Trek* made significant use of tracked music and music written for one episode and re-used in others.

MOTIFS

There are reoccurring motifs that *Star Trek* viewers have come to expect and hold sacrosanct, such as Spock arching his left eyebrow each time he utters "fascinating" or is faced with an intellectual challenge or moral quandary. Spock also has his own theme song; each time he is faced with a personal or troublesome situation, whenever we see him alone in his quarters, an upper-range bass plays, along with wind instruments. There is also signature soundtrack whenever there is hand-to-hand combat (congas with horns), battles with large alien vessels or creatures (made popular by "The Doomsday Machine," it reminds one of the theme song to *Jaws*), and soothing, wooing music whenever Kirk lays eyes on someone he finds attractive.

Voyeurism is constant, and becomes a narrative motif—characters watching other characters on view screens, a TV set within the television set. When Kirk and others are tested or battle aliens, the superior beings at the control helm allow the *Enterprise* crew observation via omnipresent, all-seeing camera eyes that perform close-ups and scene cuts. In "Mirror, Mirror" (4/12/68) a camera eye can find anyone on the (alternate universe) ship and disintegrate them at the push of a button. In "The Menagerie" (11/17/66 and 11/24/66) aliens project past events concerning the *Enterprise* and Captain Pike, which happens to be the original pilot, "The Cage" (1965)—in essence, those at Spock's court martial are shown a television show as produced by an alien race, but actually produced by Desilu/NBC.

INFLUENCE ON SCIENCE, LANGUAGE, AND CULTURE

A documentary, *The Science of Star Trek* (1995), essays on how the imaginative technology on the show ("Trek-nology") has become the norm of today. We need only look at the flip out cell phone and its resemblance to Federation communicators. NASA's first space shuttle was named *Enterprise* due to a letter-writing campaign by fans. Constance Penley, in *NASA/STAR TREK: Popular*

Science and Sex in America (1997), accuses NASA of intentionally appropriating and adapting *Star Trek* images, philosophy, and "ambience" to "sell" the space program to the public and Congressional oversight and funding committees. Engineers, scientists, doctors, and astronauts publicly claimed to have been inspired by *Star Trek* when making career choices. Stephen Hawking admits to being influenced. Spock, Uhura, and McCoy used colored square disks to operate the ships' computers; these resemble the floppy disks of today. In the May 23, 2007 issue of *The Stanford Review*, an article titled "'Star Trek'-type scans may reveal tumor genetics" discusses new technology being developed at the School of Medicine of the University of California, San Diego where

> by looking at images from radiological scans [...] radiologists can discern most of the genetic activity of a tumor. Such information could lead to diagnosing and treating patients individually, based on unique characteristics of their disease [...] In some ways, the work brings to mind a device that science fiction fans may recall from the TV series, "Star Trek." (n.p.)

Laser surgery, automatic doors, voice commanded technology, and talking computers were innovations later incorporated into every day use.

In *Consumer Tribes* (2007), marketing researcher Robert V. Kozinets devotes a chapter entitled "Inno-tribes:

Star Trek as Wikimedia" to this social phenomenon of television's influence as "tribal reclamation" that "is no mere throwaway b-school jargon" (194) and a field of serious study in social science. Kozinets breaks *Star Trek* fans down by region and interest—fan groups from certain cities or states, or who prefer one series to the other, or choose Klingon or Vulcan philosophy and lifestyle. Kozinets contends that these are essentially tribes in every anthropological sense. These tribes come together digitally on Internet fan sites[5] or physically at conventions; they integrate and get along or have disputes and arguments the way any tribe would. These *Star Trek* tribes have their own rules, rituals, and loyalties; one member may leave a tribe and join another; relationships, marriages, and children are byproducts. During Bill and Hilary Clinton's 1996 Whitewater scandal and trial, a bookbindery employee named Barbara Adams served as an alternate juror; Adams wore a black and red Starfleet Command uniform to court. Adams was dismissed from the trial for conducting a sidewalk interview with *American Journal*. News media reported she was dismissed for wearing her *Star Trek* attire. Adams notes, in the documentaries *Trekkies* and *Trekkies II*, the judge was supportive of her because she wore the uniform to represent her belief in the principles expressed in *Star Trek*—tolerance, peace, and faith in mankind, values the judge considered suitable for a court of law.

The Vulcan split finger "V" symbol and the phrase "live long and prosper" has integrated itself into contemporary culture; one does not need to be a fan to know where the hand gesture comes from and the semiotics associated with Mr. Spock and the Vulcan society. Other phrases such as "He's dead, Jim!" and "Are you out of your Vulcan mind?!" have appeared on T-shirts, coffee mugs, bumper stickers, and referenced in other television shows and comedy sketches. "Beam me up, Scotty" is perhaps the most commonly used; however, the phrase was never actually said in any episode—it is derived from "Beam us up, Scotty" in the animated series. Nevertheless, "Beam me up, Scotty" is a unit of our cultural lexicon, provided by the *Star Trek* phenomenon. István Csicsery-Ronay, Jr., in his essay "Escaping *Star Trek*," notes that if

> television has become the defining medium of [science fiction's] third generation, then no other text can compare with *Star Trek*—it is, as so many of its fans claim, an origin, a point where [science fiction] is born again [...] There are bookshelves of testimonies about the effect *Star Trek* has had in creating an imaginary space for difference [...] Its motifs and phrases have become ubiquitous in everyday discourse. (504)

These books Csicsery-Ronay refers to, popular and academic alike, address subtext and message in the show, such as Thomas Richards' *The Meaning of Star Trek* (1997) and Lawrence M. Krauss' *The Physics of Star Trek* (1995) which, with a foreword by Stephen Hawking, contends all the high tech on the show is feasible in today's understanding of physical science. Athena Andreadis' *To Seek Out New Life: The Biology Star Trek* (1996) examines the varieties of alien life and their biological differences from human beings—there are shape-shifting aliens, aliens made of rock, aliens made of plants, giant single cell entities floating in space, invisible aliens, lizard aliens, aliens that live in extreme heat an aliens that live in other dimensions. Is such fictional life possible within current views of physics and biology? The answer is yes. *Religions of Star Trek* (2001) by Ross M. Kraemer, William Cassidy, and Susan L. Schwartz considers beliefs beyond Earth's Judeo-Christian, Western faiths, from Vulcan (onto)logical spiritualism to the Klingons' belief of an afterlife similar to Scandinavian concepts of Odin and Valhalla (their savior, Kayless, prophecies a second coming much like Jesus, but preaches a code of warrior violence, not peace and turning the other cheek). In *Boldly Live as You've Never Lived Before: (Unauthorized and Unexpected) Life Lessons from Star Trek* (1995), Richard Raben and Hiyaguah Choen explore the effects *Star Trek* has on kids and teenagers growing up and adopting the philosophies of heroism (Kirk), codes of honor (Klingons), codes of integrity (Vulcan) and how these ideologies can be applied to every day life, such as Kirk's assertion that he does not believe in "the no-win scenario" or: one should never give up and always fight to win, by any means necessary.

In *Star Trek: The Motion Picture* (1978), Klingons speak in their own language rather than English, devised of words created by actor James Doohan and linguist Marc Okrand, later tasked to develop the language further. Okrand designed Klingonese—or "tlhIngan-Hol"—to use an object-verb-subject order, with a phonology that, while based on human natural languages, is intended to "sound" exotic and other-worldly. Paramount Pictures (which has copyrighted the language) wanted Klingonese to be guttural and harsh; Okrand wanted it to be unusual with selected sounds that are combined in ways not generally found in other languages. Klingonese has twenty-one consonants and five cardinal vowels. Orkand's *The Klingon Dictionary* (1992) and *The Klingon Way* (1995) were embraced with relish by Trekkies, resulting in a curious subculture within fandom: people speaking the language and recreating—or engaging in simulation of hyper-reality— Klingon culture and rituals, as represented in the movies and *The Next Generation*, into their everyday lives. The Klingon Language Institute has been formed, and Klingonese has been offered in several university linguistics departments across the country as an elective course and example of artificial language. Judith Hermans posted, online, her M.A. thesis from Tilberg University, titled "Klingon and its Users: A Sociolinguistics Profile."[6] Hermans studies the anthropological oddity of a fictional language becoming a part of reality. The July 29, 1999 issue of *The Onion* ran an article on a Modern Language Association report which claimed

> speakers of the *Star Trek*-based Klingon language outnumber individuals fluent in Navajo by a margin of more than seven-to-one. "Navajo, a 3,000-year-old Native American tonal language belonging to the Athabaskan/Na-Dené group of tongues, is clearly dying and will likely be extinct by 2010," MLA president Frederick Toback said. "Fortunately, though, the sad, steady decline of this once-proud Native American tongue has been more than offset by a rising interest in Klingon culture."

Hamlet, *Gilgamesh*, and *Much Ado About Nothing* have been translated and published in Klingonese, alongside the English versions; the Klingon Translation Project has converted portions of *The Bible* for the Klingon Christian. Fans dress as Klingons and Vulcans, address one another by alien names, and enact complex, detailed rituals at *Star Trek* at conventions, often in alien language.[7]

The foregoing shows how *Star Trek*, unlike any television show before or after it, has had empirical influence, outside the television set, on technology, philosophy, language, mainstream culture and fan sub-culture. The biggest development, however, is the buying and selling of material objects, where capitalism usurps *Star Trek*'s message of equality and democracy.

CONSUMER BEHAVIOR

What the *Star Trek* franchise enjoys most from loyal fans is their money, mostly in the form of merchandise acquisition and exchange. Kozinets notes, in his ethnographic study, "Utopian Enterprise: Articulating the Meanings of *Star Trek*'s Culture of Consumption," that *Star Trek* is "the greatest consumption phenomenon of our time [...] and has accounted for billions of dollars of licensed revenue" (67). Kozinets points out that fans have gone from mere viewers to members of a niche in consumer culture, buying action figures, collector cards, posters, DVDs, prop replicas, starship models, clothing, and books that "provide influential meaning and practices that structure consumers' identities, actions, and relationships" (67). The merchandizing phenomenon started with *Star Wars*.[8] Before that, collecting toys and models was a hobby for niche fans; it is now an obsession, a business, and investment opportunity for a majority. Items are often released in limited editions and their value increases over the years. Kozinets contends the "culture of consumption is used to conceptualize a particular interconnected system of commercially produced images, texts, and objects that particular groups use [...] to make collective sense of their environments and to orient their members experiences and lives" (68). In the field of sociology, one assignation of meaning that is appropriate to Kozinets is known as "symbolic interactionism." Designed by sociologist Herbert Blumer (see Blumer, 1969) symbolic interactionism is the study of how people create meaning in their lives, how people act on these meanings, and how these meanings are agreed upon by. The *Star Trek* fan may equate self-worth and self-image to what *Star Trek* items, clothing, and collectibles are owned, are affordable, and are shown to fellow fans as evidence of various levels of "fan seriousness"—that is: "I'm a bigger fan than you are because I have invested more in the material objects." A fan with the most acquisitions and possessions holds a higher "rank" (like a Starfleet captain over a lieutenant) within the fan community, or *inno-tribe*. As an ethnographer, Kozinets spent three years "in the field" infiltrating and studying *Star Trek* consumers at several conventions, "colored by my own personal history as a devoted viewer," where he can "observe and understand the actual behavior or 'perspective in action' [...] of *Star Trek* fans enacting consumption practices" (69). Similar to Kozinets' research of fans as "inno-tribes," the subculture is studied from an anthropological and sociological gaze, using qualitative social science research methods. "Like critical theory," Kozinets states, "one of cultural studies key problematics is to 'transform existing structures of power' [...] furthering a socialist agenda dedicating to critiquing and intervening the inequities of market capitalism" (70). Through a Marxist lens, *Star Trek* merchandizing creates a class system, the haves and have-nots—those who can afford to buy all the toys and those who cannot, enabling jealousy and contempt from the have-nots who cannot purchase merchandize they covet. The have-nots will find this inequality unfair. Thus, one fan may hate, envy, and want to hurt the wealthier fan showing off a rare buy (a prop, costume, or piece of art) with a high price tag. Another Marxist theory that comes into play is commodity fetishism—the *Star Trek* fan so desires and wants the consumer products, and feels incomplete unless the items are acquired, that these "things" become fetish objects. Karl Marx's argument (see *Capital Volume I*, 1971) is that these commodities come to possess magical qualities for the consumer, and when possessed, the initial meaning—such as the mechanical manufacturing and marketing of the commodity—becomes erased by the process of consumption. A detailed replica of a tri-corder or phaser, for instance, has its object relation as consumed product exchanged for money erased in the mind of the fan and becomes an object of great and personal meaning, a fetish that completes the fan's self-image and presentation of a fictional self to members of the inno-tribe.

Here is an example: the fan has an authentic, detailed replica of a Starfleet uniform, but does not possess the accessories, such as the phaser or tri-corder, that are equal in quality, not some cheap knock-off items meant for kids or less-serous fans. While these commodities may be expensive to obtain, the fan will not feel authentic, to herself and to others, unless these accoutrements go with the uniform. These fetish commodities are not products marketed to the fan but necessary to complete a fantasy. I have witnessed this at science-fiction, comic book, and *Star Trek* conventions; I have observed fans verbally argue and physically accost each other over merchandise and rare finds; I have seen fans break down into tears and threaten suicide because they either lost a commodity to someone else during an auction, did not find the dealer's table in time to buy a hard-to-acquire item, or did not have enough money to buy what they desire. Global issues and personal problems become meaningless—are also erased—and the fetish commodity is the focal point of reality crashing down around them.

Fiction—a TV show—influences meaning in both the deeply personal and social interaction. "When these simulations capture the imagination of a community," Kozinets concludes, "its members begin to behave in ways that authenticate the simulation so that it becomes the social reality of the community" (84). Jean Baudrillard, in *Simulations* (1983) refers to this as when "the eye of the TV is no longer the source of an absolute gaze" (52). The result becomes "the dissolution of TV into life, the dissolution of life into TV […] TV watches us, TV manipulates us" (55-56). In *The System of Objects* (1968) Baudrillard theorizes this condition as "the new morality" with "the obligation to buy" (173), something consumer *Star Trek* fans devoutly adhere to, or *disappear* into, their identities *erased*. Mundane life indeed dissolves into a televised reality that becomes an answer to the social problems of the outside world: the self vanishes into *Star Trek* subculture as fan/consumer and engages in the rejection of the human, favoring the Klingon or Vulcan. This becomes a welcome alternative to personal failures, larger economic failures, larger issues of war, famine, and rising gas prices; personal problems of employment, education, and self-esteem take a back seat; and here we have it: the 45-minute episode with four acts transformed into hyper-reality that holds more truth for the fan/consumer than the truth of their living being.

In his essay, "Suggestions for the Study of Mass-Media Effects," Harold Blumer admonishes that "studies seeking to ascertain the effects of mass media are easily led to overlook the state of sensitivity of the 'audience,' and particularly the process of collective definition that is so proverbial in shaping and sustaining the state of sensitivity" (*Symbolic Interactionism* 188). In general, Blumer refers to mass media's influence on, say, the voting habits of individuals, or their worldview of politics as fed through television and news. However, his points on mass-media influence can be used as a lens into *Star Trek* fan culture, considering the premise of symbolic interaction "is that human beings act toward things on the basis of the meanings that the things have for them" (2) and the source of these meaningful things (objects, people, concepts, religion). *Star Trek* fans collectively define themselves through their shared ascribed meanings of the show, the characters' lives, the messages in the episodes, and the objects on television that they can obtain and possess (a replica of a tri-corder, a scale model of a starship). Blumer further states that studies "of the effects of mass media-influence should seek to reflect accurately the empirical world in which the influence is operating" and "any given media influence should be studied in relation to other influences which they may be operating in the area of concern" (192). *Star Trek* fans—likewise fans of *Star Wars, Lord of the Rings,* and other science-fiction movies, television shows, or books—are often ridiculed and stigmatized by people who do not share the obsession, or even interest. "Fan boys" and "geeks" and "nerds" are often terms ascribed to them. In junior high and high school, fans are often outcast, made fun of, yet they seek each other out and form clubs; they share common interests. The grouping expands in the fan world; as adults, the fans come to terms with the meaning fandom has for them, and they are not afraid to publicly express this. Blumer calls for studies to consider other influences in the empirical world—in this case, what happens in the lives of people that draw them to become so immersed into the *Star Trek* universe that it translates into something that is more important than reality? What are the outside factors of a person's life that is the root of their escaping into a science-fiction setting, where watching, and reading, *Star Trek* goes beyond a mere hour's worth of escapist entertainment but begins to shape their lives, their philosophy, their desires? The reasons widely vary—social awkwardness, dysfunctional family, a fear of world events; whatever the reason is, to use Blumer's methods of understanding is to consider all the influences in a fan's life, beyond just the desire to become a Vulcan or Klingon, to wish that *Star Trek* was real and they could leave earth.

In a *Saturday Night Live* skit, William Shatner makes an appearance at a *Star Trek* convention; during a Q&A session with fans dressed as aliens and Starfleet officers, Shatner (playing the simulacra of himself representing the fictional Captain Kirk) blurts:

> Having received all your letters over the years, and I've spoken to many of you, and some of you have traveled—y'know—hundreds of miles to be here, I'd just like to say...GET A LIFE, will you people? I mean, for crying out loud, it's just a TV show! I mean, look at you, look at the way you're dressed! You've turned an enjoyable little job, that I did as a lark for a few years, into a COLOSSAL WASTE OF TIME! [...]it's just a TV show dammit, IT'S JUST A TV SHOW![9]

Shatner pokes fun at fandom, yet he is also addressing a serious issue in the psychology of the fan and how obsession may be ruining their lives and used as a path toward denial—or, *Star Trek* is all they live for, all they believe in, and the fan loses all realization that their beliefs are based on non-reality. An example of this breakdown of fiction and fact is an incident where Harlan Ellison, speaking on a college campus, upset a member of the audience who accused Ellison of sacrilege when Ellison stated he wrote the words Spock uttered in "The City on the Edge of Forever." Ellison breached *Star Trek* mythos: shattering a communal agreement of Spock's veracity and admitting Spock is not a real person, that the Spock in the episode is a Spock that originated from Ellison's imagination. Ellison's agency over fantasy becomes a sin. As Ellison has explained in interviews and lectures, this fan could not deal with this "truth" and viewed Ellison as committing heresy against a sacrosanct belief.[10] Other fans have written, on various websites and bulletin boards, that Gene Roddenberry did not "imagine" the world of *Star Trek* as a writer but was a conduit for a galactic consciousness to reveal to earthlings what life is truly like in the universe, beyond the confines of earth and a mundane existence. Such an expansive concept of the Federation of Planets was too big and important to have been created by the mind of a mere mortal man out to make a living through entertainment; Roddenberry, certain fans contend, was influenced by aliens to spread the truth though television.

LIFE-CHANGING RESULTS

While the series was active, none of the actors could have predicted what their characters, and the show, would come to signify and how it would alter their lives and public image, *and* economic status. They have all acknowledged that at the time, *Star Trek* was simply a job, a paycheck, and not material for serious actors. Shatner, after all, was only working in television to feed his three children; he preferred to be on stage, performing Shakespeare. Two, three decades later, these actors became financially secure because of *Star Trek*, through merchandizing, appearances, memoirs, autographs, and ghost-written novels.[11] Guest stars on single or multiple episodes have enjoyed recognition and an amount of fame, sometimes reprisals of their characters on another series and the feature films (such as Spock's father, Sarek). Bit actors who played "red shirts"—the disposable characters killed in the teasers—have cashed in on the *Star Trek* money train, selling autographed photos at conventions and through the mail. An April 8, 2005 *Los Angeles Times* article, "'Star Trek' Bit Players Cling On" notes that

> Michael Dante may not be on any Hollywood A-list, but on this weekend in Pasadena, he was intergalactic. Dante was capitalizing on his appearance in a

single episode of the original "Star Trek" series. It aired Dec. 1, 1967. "But it was a very popular episode," Dante insisted, speaking in the same wooden tone he used as Maab, lead villain on the planet Capella IV. "It had action. It had comedy. It had drama."

Actress Tanya Lemani, who plays a belly dancer with no dialogue in "Wolf in the Fold" (12/22/67) admits amazement that she is known by thousands for that single role, rather than any other work she has done during her career, such as one-episode appearances on *The Flying Nun*, *Get Smart*, and *I Dream of Jeannie*. She states in interviews: "Nobody remembers anything but *Star Trek*."[12]

COMMERCIAL BREAK: NOTES

1. The tactic still works, most recently with the return of *Jericho* (CBS, 2007-08), cancelled after season one. The show was continued until a resolution of the story and various subplots were wrapped up. When networks cancel a show without completing a story arc, or bringing about an ending of events, this often negates future DVD sales; in some cases, resolutions will be filmed for the sake of a DVD boxed set, or include scripts that were not shot.

2. Nancy Sinatra and Sammy David, Jr. had kissed on a live broadcast the year before in a December 1967 musical-variety special, *Movin' with Nancy,* but they were not fictional characters, so this did not count in the history of television series broadcasting.

3. A scene in the eleventh *Star Trek* (2009) movie is shot at Vasquez Rocks as homage to the original series. The setting is iconic among fans—in *Bill and Ted's Bogus Journey* (1991), they are watching the episode "Arena" and then transported there by their evil robot replicas. The fans in *Free Enterprise* (1991) re-enact the episode there. Other television series with Vasquez Rocks locations include *The Rifleman, Bonanza, 24,* and *CSI.*

4. This sound was created vocally by Alexander Courage. This was pre-synthesizer times.

5. Kozinets also coined the term "netnography" for the ethnographic study of internet culture.

6. See http://www.geocities.com/judith_hh/scripdef.htm. See also http://www.judion.de/klingon/

7. Hermans writes, "Volapük is another artificial language. Many Esperantists spoke this language before turning to Esperanto. Volapük was the creation of Monsignor Johann Martin Schleyer, a German parish priest. He was said to have known in one fashion or another 83 languages. The invention of Volapük, as he says himself, happened while he was suffering from insomnia." The artificial language in James Joyce's *Finnegans Wake* is also spoken by Joyce fans to one another. Each summer, I attend the International ComicCon in San Diego. I have since I was twelve, and one of the highlights, which started in the early 1990s, is a Klingon theater piece performed by the Klingon Society. Each year it is different, from the Ascension ritual (when a Klingon male becomes an adult warrior), to a trial of a Federation officer, to a "traditional" Klingon wedding, or a re-enactment of an adventure. Fans line up by the hundreds—the thousands—to watch these performances, often spoken in a combination of English and Klingonese. Parents dress their children as small Klingons. The costumes and make up are elaborate and highly detailed, either comparable to what is seen on TV and film or sometimes even better.

8. George Lucas foresaw this market. When *Star Wars* went over budget and he needed more funding to complete the movie, he agreed to a considerable pay cut for himself, in exchange for

all merchandizing rights and creative control of sequels. Since 20th Century Fox was not optimistic about the success of *Star Wars*, the company agreed, a decision regretted to this day (the contract was solid and unbreakable, as much as the studio's lawyers sought out loopholes to manipulate years later); Lucas has earned tens of millions of dollars off of merchandise alone.

9. http://snltranscripts.jt.org/86/86hgetalife.phtml

10. I base this information on one of Ellison's lectures I attended in 1998.

11. It is no secret that Shatner's *Star Trek* offshoot and *Tek Wars* novels are ghost-written.

12. See http://tanyalemani.com/

ACT II

ALIEN SEX FIENDS, AMOROUS ADROIDS, AND INTERSELLAR PROMISCUITY

THE ERA

To place *Star Trek* into a proper critical context, we must consider the political and social changes that occurred when the show was broadcast, and how the episodes were influenced by, and reflected, the world outside the fiction. The late 1960s were tough times for TV programming and *Star Trek*, set in a universe where there is a single earth government, under the umbrella of a galactic "Federation" of planets and alien races, with the Federation's headquarters placed in San Francisco, California.[1] The nations of the Earth live and work together in peace, having survived a few devastating global wars—these wars are never fully explained, but in *Star Trek: First Contact* (1996), mid-twenty-first-century Earth is left devastated and nations splintered after a global nuclear engagement, and the creation of warp drive technology, and contact with the Vulcans, helps bring the people of earth together in apparent utopian harmony. Such positive and democratic visions of the future did not quell with the turmoil of the 1960s, at least not with corporate America. The Vietnam conflict was in full swing; there was violence on university campuses and riots in major cities; people were afraid of nuclear bombs, communists, spies. Those under the age of thirty did not share the same worldview as the previous generations and those in power within government, broadcasting, and advertising, three entities that influence (and decide) whether a television show makes or breaks it in the world of commerce. There was also the sexual revolution going on: embraced by one side of America, condemned by the other. *Star Trek* attempted to show a future where all the current problems of the day had been conquered; where enemies were non-human and lived in outer space rather than next door; where men and women were "equal" and whenever there was conflict and danger, mankind always walked away, taking the high road, victorious, righteous, and strong. At least, that was Roddenberry's original intent—what was represented in various episodes seemed to stray from that.

THE FEMALE IMAGE

The women in *Star Trek* are fiercely independent, dress provocatively, their roles widely varied: from ranking officers, doctors, world leaders, formidable enemies and assassins, to slaves, seductresses, and catalysts of destruction. This was a radical departure for the roles women played in most television shows at the time: the mother and happy homemaker, devoted and obedient wife (think June Cleaver in *Leave It to Beaver*); or the secretary, prostitute, and victim (pretty much any crime show had them, solved by male detectives). Shows such as *That Girl* and *The Flying Nun* attempted to expand on the representation of women's roles in the late 1960s.

The uniforms worn by women serving on board the *Enterprise* are basically mini-dresses and barely cover their hips, sometimes revealing panty shots and always a good deal of nylon-covered leg (in the spin-offs, women and men wear the same single-piece red or blue attire). Other women—human and alien alike—wear sheer, light, revealing outfits, exposing skin (pink, brown, or green), mid-drifts, ample cleavage, and rear ends. The executives and producers knew the science fiction demographic well: young men with active hormones and an appreciation of the female form…this is the same reason that many science-fiction novels and magazines often had, and still have, women in sexy outfits on the covers, even if the image has nothing to do with the contents.

In her on-line article "Sex and the *Star Trek* Woman," Laura Goodwin contends that feminists do not have a negative critical view of *Star Trek*'s portrayal of women, and that it was not a sexist show. It was in fact an anti-sexist show. In TOS, women were respected, and well represented. We met female queens, priestesses, soldiers, warriors, villains, and heroines. Virtually all of the *Star Trek* women had careers, and were self-supporting [....] It's pretty clear that TOS-era men and women are 100% casual about the sight of women's bare legs, to such an extent that the military issues these skimpy uniforms. [2]

Other critics disagree. "That the original *Star Trek* was sexist hardly needs articulation," contends Elyce Rae Helford in her essay, "A Part of Myself No Man Should Ever See," adding: "Feminist critics attack the stereotypical femininity of the series' women, the oversexualization or demonization of the few competent female characters, and the eroticization of women of color" (11). Helford reads the final episode, "Turnabout Intruder" (6/29/69) as Kirk's repressed feminine side taking over and his masculine resistance which wins the gender battle and represents a sexist message that men are greater than women. Edward Whetmore maintains the same view in her essay, "A Female Captain's Enterprise," suggesting the *Enterprise* may have been better off commanded by a Kirk with a woman's soul, who would make less violent choices, or think twice about interfering with an alien culture's society. "Turnabout Intruder" has sparked more critical discourse on gender and inequality than any other episode. Although *The Next Generation* had women in the role of Starfleet Admirals and *Voyager* had a tough, no-nonsense female captain, the original series will always be criticized for its portrayal of women as sex objects, evident in Karin Blair's "Sex and *Star Trek*," Ann Cranny-Francis' "Sexuality and Sex-Role Stereotyping in *Star Trek*," and Mary Ann Tetreault's "The Trouble with *Star Trek*," that outline the faults of power and position in the futuristic military, contending that the women in the show are merely eye candy for the men in charge and the male-centric fans. In "Miri" (6/29/67), for instance, Yeoman Rand becomes a victim of her attractiveness: she breaks into tears and confesses to Kirk that she feels unattractive of the aging disease the landing party has contracted, the effects appearing on her legs. She is ashamed of her legs, and admits that on the *Enterprise,* she tried to make Kirk look at her long, shapely gams. Perhaps Goodwin is correct: so much leg is taken for granted onboard a twenty-third-century space ship, and not considered "sexy" in twentieth-century terms. Goodwin suggests that Rand only wants Kirk to see her as a woman, not as an equal or an officer; that the needs and insecurities between the sexes has not changed much in the future. Other critics will view this as a weakness on Rand's part—this shows her desire to please her boss, submitting to his base masculinity, and drawing viewers' sexual attention to her legs rather than her role as an officer.

CAPTAIN KIRK'S LIBIDO

Captain James T. Kirk's sexual exploits have been a long-running joke and point of contention in *Star Trek* mythos. Viewers have guffawed, admired, and been appalled by the Captain's macho methods of saving the galaxy, taking off his shirt and showing off his physique whenever the opportunity arises (which he does from the start in "The Man Trap"); romancing every human, alien, or android female that guest stars in an episode; falling in love and, in three cases, having his heart broken and soul shattered by the death of that love. The first greatest loss is Edith Keeler in "The City on the Edge of Forever," discussed in Act III. The second is an American-Indian-like woman/alien he marries after a head injury and amnesia, believing he is a god called "Kurak" in "The Paradise Syndrome" (10/4/68); this wife is also several weeks pregnant, so he loses two lives connected dear him. The third is an android female in "Requiem for Methuselah" (2/14/69); she malfunctions and short-circuits when she feels deep and painful love for Kirk and does not know how to process the strange (post human) emotions. Kirk's grief over her is so great that Spock uses a Vulcan mind-meld that causes Kirk to forget her.

He has also had a fair share of women from his past who come home to roost—Dr. Janice Lester in "The Turnabout Intruder" who switches her soul with his, so that she inhabits his body; Dr. Carol Marcus in *Star Trek II: The Wrath of Kahn* (1982), who bore him a son he never had the chance to know, the son later murdered by a Klingon in *Star Trek III: The Search for Spock* (1985). In "Court-Martial" (2/2/67) the lawyer from the Federation's judge advocate general's office is a former girlfriend, and prosecutes Kirk; in "Shore Leave" (12/29/66), Kirk remembers fondly of a past flame from his Academy days and a psychic planetary computer manufactures a simulacrum body that imitates her. Captain Kirk's penis is busy in the twenty-third century and other centuries he visits when time traveling. Pocket Books canonizes this fact with the publication of *Captain Kirk's Guide to Women* (2008), and this jacket copy: "Casanova, Don Juan, James Bond these are men of legendary romance, but only one man can boast that his seductive powers take him boldly *where no man has gone before:* James T. Kirk."

Kirk is a man who does not like to lose, does not believe in the "no-win scenario" referred to as the "Kobayashi-Maru" test in *Wrath of Kahn*, a Starfleet Academy test that has no positive, winning outcome—it is a test of character and mettle for potential command officers (we learn that Kirk, as a cadet, cheated and reprogrammed the test so he could win, getting "an accommodation for original thinking"). He always saves the Galaxy and never fails in this endeavor; he is attractive to the opposite sex for his prowess and power; and he expects the sexual conquests that are the end result. He would not know what to do if a woman said "no." Kirk's salad days seems to be the period when he was a Starfleet cadet to the five-year mission. There are two occasions where Kirk does not seek the amorous attentions of a woman and *he* falls in love with *them* due to biochemistry: in "A Private War" (2/2/68) Kirk is bitten by an alien beast and the only way to cure him from the poison is for a local woman who practices herbal "witchcraft" to use a special root that mixes their blood and, according to her, connects their souls. Kirk falls into a drugged-like daze, beholden to her. The same happens in "Elaan of Troyius" (12/20/68)—Elaan's touch can make a man emotionally enslaved to her; when she cries and a tears contact Kirk's flesh, he goes to mush.

There are two incidents of Kirk's ability to make the opposite sex swoon that were controversial. Sadomasochist imagery in "The Gamesters of Triskelion" (1/13/68), where Kirk, Uhura, and Chekov are kidnapped and forced to become gladiators for three bored disembodied brains that are entertained by observing their captives fight and mate; these slaves wear "collars of obedience" and outfits with an S/M fashion flair. Kirk is paired off with a barely-clothed silver-haired woman with ample breasts[3] and long legs; her role is fight trainer and bed companion. He intentionally makes her fall in love with him as they spend time together in their shared cage, so she will rebel against the games masters. This disobedience against her masters nearly kills her. Next, a Lolita complex and shades of pedophilia are subtext in "Miri," where Kirk intentionally uses his charms to make nymphet Miri (who is thirteen or fourteen) fall for him and do his bidding. He compliments her with a soothing voice and tells her how beautiful he is. She absorbs this attention because she is lonely, and a female needing attention. We later learn Miri is actually three hundred years old, so Kirk is romancing an older woman, not a girl, for all intents.

Love and lust in the *Star Trek* universe are liberated. We have to view the show's treatment of sensuality within context of the so-called "sexual revolution," but today we must also question how progressive Roddenberry's utopian future truly is. If Kirk behaved as he does in today's military command structure, he would have a short career, plagued with sexual harassment charges, reduction in rank, loss of command due to incompetence, and quite possibly court-martial and a dishonorable discharge for amoral acts unbecoming of an officer.

Consider Yeoman Rand, Kirk's attractive, feisty, personal assistant at the top of season one. She wears the obligatory mini-dress uniform and has long blonde hair bundled up in a Sixties-style beehive "do." At first Kirk is uncomfortable with having a female yeoman assigned to him—she brings him his lunch and dinner, pays attention to his diet, waits on his every need. Other officers are envious and gleefully snicker in hushed voices, insinuating that Rand may provide other, less regulatory service to her Captain. Rand goes on away missions and is a strong presence in the first half of season one, but later fades into the shadows, appearing sporadically with few lines of dialogue. There does seem to be a relationship developing between her and Kirk, perhaps never consummated or discussed. In "Mirror, Mirror," however, when Kirk notices another Yeoman on the *Enterprise*, whom he has never met before but his alternate universe self had a serious relationship with her alternate universe self, his interest in piqued; in the coda, we see Kirk coyly sliding up alongside this Yeoman and engaging her in flirtatious conversation. His pursuit of any type of relationship with a female subordinate is plagued by unequal power; if a female crew member does not find him attractive, it is unlikely she is going to brush her Captain off. One may surmise that Kirk's repeated knack for courting and conquering women on other ships and planets—humanoid or otherwise—would be of concern for that generally invisible governmental body "Starfleet Command." It could be that sexual harassments lawsuits have been done away with in Roddenberry's utopia.

Kirk is not the only senior officer practicing biology. In fact, everyone does except Sulu and Uhura (whose alternate selves both had some kind of history in the "Mirror, Mirror" universe). In "Who Mourns for Adonis?" (9/22/67), Scotty is enamored with a young female ensign and becomes extremely jealous and irrational when the Greek god, Apollo, takes an interest in her and she reciprocates. So deep is his jealousy that Scotty nearly gets himself killed, knowing very well that he is no match for an all-powerful deity. In "The Lights of Zetar" (1/31/69), Scotty quickly falls in love with a scientist and makes foolish choices again.[4]

In "Shore Leave" (12/29/66), Dr. McCoy has a budding relationship with Ensign Tonia Barrows. She becomes jealous when McCoy, after being killed, rises from the dead, "repaired," with two "dancers" that resemble Playboy Bunnies on each arm.[5] In "For the World is Hollow and I Have Touched the Sky" (11/8/68), McCoy finds a humanoid-alien woman to love and marry; she lives inside a hollow asteroid that is also a vast ship. McCoy has contracted an incurable disease and only has a year to live. He decides to leave the *Enterprise* and spend his last days in his wife's arms.[6]

Mr. Chekov runs into a former girlfriend in "The Way to Eden" (2/29/69), referred to by fans as "Hippies in Space." Irina Galilulin is a scantily-clad fellow Russian national he was involved with back in the Academy; she dropped out for an alternative hippie-like lifestyle while he remained in the military. Chekov is not always the young Casanova, however; in "Day of the Dove" (11/1/68) he is possessed by a violent alien entity and attempts to rape a Klingon woman. He proves to be a fool for love, much like Scotty, when he falls for a woman that does not exist—a simulacrum created by an alien intelligence—in "Spectre of the Gun" (10/25/68).

Mr. Spock, suppressing all emotions of his human half, has the most complicated love life of them all. Nurse Chapel has an impassioned crush on Spock but can never get herself to verbalize her desire. Spock is aware of her feelings yet never discourages her, sometimes giving her mixed signals. When Chapel finds out that Spock has a Vulcan woman that he has been betrothed to since childhood in "Amok Time" (9/15/67) —Vulcans engage in the act of arranged marriages to create power families—her heart sinks.[7] "Amok Time" reveals the sexual cycles of Vulcan males, when they lose all sense of logic and have the burning need to mate every seven years—the *Pon Farr*—and must do so or die in celibate madness and agony. In "This Side of Paradise" (3/2/67), Lelia Kalomi, who once had futile feelings for the love-challenged Spock when the two knew each other on a different planet, exposes him to the spores of a plant on Omicron Ceti III. The spores alter his physiology, causes his human side to emerge. We witness a carefree, playful Spock in love. We also get a glimpse of a deeply serious, lustful, violent Spock in "All Our Yesterdays" (3/14/69), when, traveling back 6000 years in time, he reverts to the ways of his barbaric ancestors. He is seduced by a woman, Zarabeth; all Spock wants to do is have sex and eat animal flesh (contemporary Vulcans are vegetarians).

THE SIMULACRUM AND THE SUPERIOR BEING

"It is my impression that your race is not yet ready to understand us," claims the Caretaker on the "Shore Leave" planet. This is a common statement made by advanced races throughout the series, as if humankind is nothing more than simple-minded barbarians who somehow stumbled onto interstellar technology. The peaceful but all powerful Organians, in "Errand of Mercy" (3/23/67) claim they are far too advanced for human and Klingon minds to comprehend. The Metrons in "Arena" (1/19/67) inform Kirk that the Federation is not ready to interact with their race, but notes that humanity "shows promise," and "maybe in a few thousand years" the two races can engage in a dialogue. The Metrons are impressed when Kirk does not resort to violence to solve an issue, as are the Melkots in "Spectre of the Gun," who believe humans are too sadistic for first contact; they place Kirk and crew into a fabricated O.K. Corral to re-enact a mythical wild west gunfight; Kirk and company pass the "test" when they refuse to participate in the bloodshed. A superior being testing mankind was one of Roddenberry's pet recurring themes. In "The Corbomite Maneuver," the ghoulish alien Belloch threatens to destroy the *Enterprise* but turns out to be a puppet, a "man behind the curtain," operated by a three-foot-tall being (played by a child). In "The Menagerie" Parts 1 and 2, large-headed telepathic aliens test mankind's array of emotions, alien to them—love, fear, hate—by setting up an illusionary world with their collective minds.

Not all the advanced races are benevolently self-righteous. Trelane from "The Squire of Gothos" (1/12/67) is a pompous and devious omniscient super being who wants to "play" with Kirk and crew. He puts Kirk on "trial" for his actions—the twist is that Trelane (portrayed by an actor in his late 30s) is actually a child; his parents tell him to put away his "pets" or else he will "not be permitted to make any more planets." The parents are two well-mannered disembodied voices that appear as shimmering lights; they apologize to Kirk about their child's inconsiderate behavior to lower life forms because "we indulge him too much." The rock-based aliens Excalibans create simulacrums of Abraham Lincoln, Genghis Kahn, and other historical figures to wage battle with one another in order to understand the concept of "good vs. evil" in "The Savage Curtain" (3/7/69).

Jean Baudrillard was formulating his theory of the simulacra around the time *Star Trek* was in re-runs. Norman K. Denzin, in *Images of Postmodern Society* (1991), writes that "the simulacrum, which means an image, the semblance of an image, make-believe, or that which conceals the truth or the real [...] is a central concept in Baudrillard's theory of history" (30). *Star Trek* is populated with simulated life, doubles, replacements and doppelgangers. Kirk has been split in two from a transporter malfunction, had an android copy made of him, and fallen in love with a manufactured human being that he thought was real. The transporter is a technology that essentially creates simulations, or copies, of the source material; Dr. McCoy often expresses his dislike for teleportation, having his atoms blasted into a million pieces and then reassembled does not sit well with the doctor. The transporter is able to filter out and remove any germs, viruses, and biological hazards attached to a landing party's body, thus removing the need for quarantine every time someone goes down on an alien planet where there are alien microbes.

Two questions arise: (1) After teleportation, is the body still the original, or a re-made body, a filtered copy, that beams back to the ship? (2) What else can be removed from a body, and what can be added, via the transporter? In *Star Trek: The Motion Picture* two people suffer from a transportation malfunction: their insides are beamed onto their outsides, rendered to a pile of intestines, organs, and meaty flesh. In "Mirror, Mirror," an ion storm causes the transporter to send the landing party into an alternate universe. With all these constant malfunctions—killing, creating doppelgangers or new life forms, or sending people into a 180-degree opposite reality—why do they even take the risk?

Roddenberry conceived teleportation as a means to keep production costs down—it would be too complicated to have a ship the size of the *Enterprise* land on planets and show the characters emerge form the vessel, and during filming, the models for shuttlecrafts were often not ready by production dates, so Roddenberry imagined that it would be easier, and cheaper, to just have bodies instantly appear on locations.

SPACE AGE IMPERIALISM

Starfleet officers abides by a "Prime Directive," a law of non-interference with the natural evolution of any alien species or society, yet there are numerous incidents that operate against the mandate, often perpetrated by Captain Kirk's choice and belief that he is doing more good than harm. For instance, in "A Piece of the Action," (1/12/88), the people of the planet Iotia, who imitate other cultures rather than having one of their own, have been strangely influenced by early Starfleet explorers 100 years prior: the crew of the *U.S.S. Horizon* accidentally left behind a 1992 edition of an academic study, *Chicago Mobs of the Twenties*, that the Iotians took as a cultural text to appropriate. The result: an entire planet based solely on early twentieth-century Chicago and run by clichéd gangsters toting Tommy guns, with stereotypical mob bosses, each with an alluring "moll" at his side. The episode has its comic moments and is rendered even more absurd by being, or attempting to be, serious toward the fourth act. Kirk takes it upon himself to interfere with the culture and forces the Federation implied might by bringing all the mob bosses together. Kirk coerces them into forming a consortium to end the violence and turf wars, to make decisions democratically, and to share in the profits of trade. He justifies this by using twenty-third-century Earth as an example, where all the resisting nations have unified. Kirk threatens that the Federation will drop in unannounced to collect their share of profits, their "piece of the action," although Kirk has no intention of doing that. In the coda, he finds his forced change of the Iotian culture amusing.

In "Patterns of Force" (1/15/68) the planet Ekos is contaminated by the native aliens misconstruing the ideas of twentieth-century Nazi Germany introduced by ethnographer John Gill, who (drugged up by his puppet masters) becomes the "Fuehrer of the Fatherland." The neighboring planet, Zeon, become the Jews whom the simulacra Nazis must destroy. Kirk decides to interfere (since interference has already happened by Gill) and expose the Führer's true identity. While it appears that Kirk has engaged in a righteous act (after all, Nazis are evil from a historical human context), many people die (including Gill) and Kirk never considers how much death will come from resistance to change and the revelation of truth. There is no evidence to support Kirk's interference will have a positive outcome. The two races have been at violent odds for many generations, what makes Kirk believe that he has instantly "fixed" what was "wrong"? In "Bread and Circuses" (3/18/68), a planet fashions itself after the Roman Empire, with gladiator games; the contamination comes form (again) a crashed Starfleet vessel, with the survivors setting themselves up as Senators in this new Rome; there is an underground resistance movement, the worshippers of the sun, which Kirk and crew later figure out is "the son," or the son of God, as in Jesus.[8] It appears the survivors of the crash contaminated the planet's culture with Earth-based Christianity. One again, Kirk takes it upon himself to eschew the Prime Directive and topple the ruling structure of the Roman simulacra government and its polytheism, to make way for monotheism and "the son," never glancing back on Earth history to note such acts is often the seed of genocide and war.

A separate view of Kirk's actions: *Star Trek* represented counter-culture thinking of the 1960s and a spreading desire among America's younger generation to topple existing authority and institutions of government and religion. Kirk does just that many times: he destroys the ruling government bodies, the ruling computer or god, or dismantles the social system of alien cultures that he finds oppressive and anti-democratic. In this manner, *Star Trek* becomes an *American* television show that posits American worldviews; "universal English" is the common language in the Federation, thus American influence expands off the Earth and across the Galaxy. In the episode "The Omega Glory" (3/1/68), the *Enterprise* answers a distress call from the *U.S.S. Exeter*—the ship is devoid of life, the crew had contracted a disease on the planet it orbits. On the surface of Omega IV, the *Exeter*'s sole survivor, Captain Ron Tracey, has blatantly violated the Prime Directive by introducing phaser technology to a group of humanoids called the "Kohms," who have Asian/Mongol features; their sworn enemies are Caucasian "barbarians" called the "Yangs." Tracy has altered the balance of natural power; Kirk exhibits shocked and outraged that his colleague has defied Starfleet's top mandate, regardless of his own transgressions in the past (that Kirk is apparently in denial of). They soon discover that the inhabitants of Omega IV have a mirrored history to twentieth-century Earth, engaged in a Cold War of their own—the "Kohms" reflect Communists and "Yangs" Yankees. The Yangs worship "Old Glory," a tattered American flag; their prayers to Old Glory are a truncated, distorted version of "The Pledge of Allegiance." Inside a sacred box: a parchment copy of the Declaration of Independence, meant only for the eyes of gods. The Yangs consider Kirk a God because he knows their prayer words and can recite, verbatim, the opening of the Declaration (done so with a patriotic soundtrack): if he knows the holy semiotics, the natives declare Kirk a deity, bow to the ground, and pledge their enslavement to his will.[9] Kirk informs—"educates"—the Yangs that the Declaration was not meant for gods but for all men, equal in a free society. Kirk, as he has done before, deconstructs and destroys the religious beliefs of another culture, replacing it with human (and Starfleet's, or in this case, America's) ideology.

Kirk's confidence in his actions possesses a serious flaw: by Tracy's influence, the culture has evolved a certain way, and that evolution is now natural; by imposing change, and convincing the Yangs and Kohms that their societal structure has been erroneously tampered with— that is, telling the dumb natives they are *wrong*—Kirk himself now interferes with the culture's continued evolution. Like the tribal people in "The Apple" (10/13/67), whose god is killed by Kirk (discussed below), these beings *have no other choice but to accept Kirk's point of view.*

ARTIFICIAL INTELLIGENCE

"The Ultimate Computer" (3/8/68) comments on the fears of humans becoming obsolete on a starship that can be run by one main super computer, the "M-5," constructed by Dr. Daystrom. The M-5, similar to Hal2000 from *2001: A Space Odyssey* (1968), malfunctions and becomes both autonomous and homicidal because Daystrom imprinted his personality into the hardware. He did this to fix the faults in the previous four versions of the computer programming. Daystrom is on the verge of a nervous breakdown; that part of his personality translates into the algorithms, a digital (or in this case, analog) schizophrenia. This melding of computer hardware and human software becomes a cautionary tale of too much reliance on technology and automatons, even in an advanced spacefaring society. Kirk outsmarts M-5 by pointing out the computer's errors, causing the M-5 to systematically break down (much like its creator has psychologically) when it realizes it is not perfect.

There are several episodes of androids imitating humans so well that it is hard to tell them apart—in "I, Mudd" (11/3/67) opportunist Harcourt Fenton Mudd escapes the penal colony for crimes committed during "Mudd's Women" (10/13/66) and has stumbled upon a planet populated by self-replicating androids. These artificial life forms have put him on a throne, deem him their leader; however, they will not allow him to leave the planet, or their sight. He becomes a prisoner in his own kingdom; the non-human society deprives him of the freedom to *be* human.

Computers with delusions of godhood must be dealt with, too. In "Return of the Archons" (2/9/67) and "The Apple," antediluvian mainframes have evolved into megalomaniac deities—similar to a classic *Twilight Zone* episode, "The Old Man in the Cave" (11/8/63)—demanding worship and obedience as they control the lives of human communities. Kirk and his diligent crew, concerned with all humanoids enslaved to oppressive machines, destroy the computer gods Landru and Vaal in both episodes. They leave the humanoids behind and alone to fend for themselves—cultures that have, for hundreds of years, relied on their machine god, now abandoned by their "saviors" the Federation to form new meanings of reality. Kirk once again justifies his actions—these people will certainly have better lives without a computer telling them what to do and how to behave.

Perhaps Kirk's beliefs stem from his sharp mind and spontaneous wit; he is capable of out-thinking nefarious computers and insane robots. He finds loopholes in the programming of both Nomad from "The Changeling" (9/29/67) and the M-5. Nomad's programming directs it to destroy anything that is imperfect. Kirk presents a problem in the logic of the machines: if Nomad's creator was a human being, and human beings are imperfect, then Nomad is by default also imperfect; after all, an imperfect life form cannot create a perfect artificial intelligence. This conundrum creates confusion in the computations and Nomad enters into a feedback-loop state, eventually self-destructing when it cannot formulate an argument that disproves Kirk's theory. Not even Spock is crafty enough to come up with such brainy solutions. Kirk proves that humans, in the end, are wiser and stronger than any mechanical device; he resists the post human threat, confident in his (masculine) ability to wiggle out of the "no-win scenario."

COMMERCIAL BREAK: NOTES

1. In the films, the President of the Federation—often an alien—resides in San Francisco. It seems that the political might of the Galaxy revolves around San Francisco, and the United States, bringing to mind beliefs, prior to Galileo and Coperni-

cus, that the Universe, God's chosen planet, was the center of everything, and all the stars and planets revolved around the Earth.

2. See http://allyourtrekarebelongto.us/tossex.htm

3. This is commonly known as the BBB syndrome in science-fiction marketed to young men: the Big Bare Breasted female that graced the covers of novels and magazines. This marketing ploy has changed little, as BBB images are often found on the covers of high fantasy and vampire novels.

4. In *Star Trek VI: The Undiscovered Country*, there is an affectionate scene between the aging Scott and Uhura that suggests there has been a romance between the two at one point.

5. In the novels from the Pocket Books series, Barrows and McCoy continue their romance and marry; she eventually dies though.

6. This is also another episode where Kirk and Spock destroy god-computer and alter an alien society's religious beliefs.

7. In the animated series episode, "Mudd's Passion" (11/10/73), Mudd preys on Chapel's haunted desire and gives her a love potion drug that works on Spock.

8. This is the only instance in the series where Christian beliefs are brought up. One would assume that having such elements would bring up too many questions, such as: if people in the twenty-third century still have Christian beliefs in Jesus, why hasn't Jesus returned or the Apocalypse happened, and have Biblical texts been reinterpreted to fit the times, as they have been over the centuries?

9. This is the second time he has been mistaken as a deity, a commentary toward the fallacy of primitive cultures believing Eu-

ropean explorers (colonists) with their white skin and gold are gods, and how these explorers took advantage of the interpretation.

ACT III

"THE CITY ON THE EDGE OF FOREVER"

TWO VERSIONS OF ONE STORY

No other episode has had as much controversy surrounding it as "The City on the Edge of Forever," both in print and oral history, whether the story is told by those involved or by fans recounting *Star Trek* mythos. Fans consider it one of the best episodes; *TV Guide*, in 1997, ranked it number ninety-two of "TV's Best 100 Episodes." There are two versions of the storyline: the aired episode and the first draft written by Harlan Ellison, a short story writer who paid his dues in the pulp magazine market in the 1950s, and then moved to Los Angeles to work in Hollywood, where he wrote episodes of *The Young Lawyers*, *Outer Limits*, and *The Flying Nun*, among others.

Ellison wrote several novels early in his career, but mostly composed short fiction, teleplays, and screenplays.

In Chicago, he edited the second-tier men's magazine *Rouge*, often writing content under a variety of pen names, to keep his reputation as a top science-fiction writer untarnished. He was one of the leading writers of the "New Wave" movement; his widely anthologized story, "'Repent, Harlequin!' said the Ticktockman" (1965) won both the Hugo and Nebula Awards, given by science-fiction fans at Worldcon and the Science Fiction and Fantasy Writers of America (SFWA), respectively. He edited the highly praised anthology, *Dangerous Visions* (1967), considered a flagship for the turning point in provocative, experimental science-fiction, publishing new works by Kurt Vonnegut, Robert Silverberg, Ursula K. Le Guin, and other luminaries. Gene Roddenberry wished to hire "name" writers in the genre to produce quality scripts. In *The Trouble with Tribbles* (1983), David Gerrold points out that Ellison was instrumental in getting some writers to come onboard, such as Theodore Sturgeon and Norman Spinrad, whom arguably wrote some episodes that fans consider the best in quality: Sturgeon's "Amok Time" and Spinrad's "The Doomsday Machine." (Gerrold himself penned "The Trouble with Tribbles.")

Ellison's first draft of "City," at 128 pages, was far too long for a one-hour episode. It is broken down into a teaser and four acts, yet the teaser is about twelve minutes (based on a typical script page averaging out to one minute of screen time, but this is not always true) and each act is twenty-five-to-thirty minutes. An average hour-long show will generally clock in at forty-five minutes, with fifteen minutes of advertising time; so a typical teleplay runs 45-50 pages, with each act 10-15 pages long. Gerrold explains in *The World of Star Trek* (1982): "A story must be broken into an equal number of 14-minute segments, each ending with a major climax," and "the story must be structured to allow for ads" (152). Ellison was a veteran of TV writing by then and knew this; he knew his script would have to be cut down and rewritten, but he had to get the story out of his system in that first draft, "a story I was anxious to tell" (*Six Science Fiction Plays* 7). Roddenberry and his staff were pleased with the draft and planned to get it "on the boards" quickly, yet it turned into months. What followed was heated argument between writer and producer over revisions, character and dialogue changes, and the budget. Ellison claims:

> Gene's contention was that I had written a script that cost too much to film on the budget NBC had allowed [...] I contended that unnamed parties had leeched all the humanity from the story and had turned it into just another melodramatic, implausible action-adventure hour (*Plays* 8).

This is what makes the behind-the-scenes story just as interesting as the episode, and educates on how scripts evolve on their way to the small screen.

TELEVISED VERSION

The *Enterprise* is caught in the turbulence of "ripples in time" and "space displacement" while orbiting a new and uncharted planet. Mr. Sulu is injured during the commotion, causing him to have a heart flutter, and Dr. McCoy revives the helmsman with a small amount of a stimulant called cordrazine, which Kirk calls "tricky stuff" because it is a new medical drug. When the ship buckles, McCoy accidentally injects himself with a large and possibly deadly dose of the cordrazine. McCoy becomes frantic, paranoid, and hallucinatory, screaming "killers!" and "assassins!" and "I won't let you!" He knocks out the transporter chief and beams himself down to the planet, believing that his imagined enemies are out to get him. He has transported down to the center of the time disturbance. Kirk, Spock, Scotty, Uhura, and two security officers go after him. The landing party find themselves in a giant ruined city; the winds whistle around them, dust and rock are everywhere. The structures are "10,000 centuries old," according to Spock's tri-corder. They examine a structure, an oval-shaped sculpture, doughnut-like in its appearance, made of glowing rock and metal. The portal calls itself The Guardian of Time, and claims to have been there "since the beginning of time." The Guardian states it is a "gateway to your own past" and shows them televised-like, black and white images of earth's history. Spock is recording it all in his tri-corder, which will be important later on.

McCoy, still caught up in his madness, jumps through the portal and "passes through what once was," says the Guardian. The *Enterprise* cannot be raised on communicators. McCoy has changed history somehow. It is up to Kirk and Spock to save earth, the Federation, the galaxy, and "attempt to set right" history. The two jump into the portal, having no idea if they have gone to the correct time and place. They find themselves in New York City in 1930s, during the Depression. The set is a studio back lot, with storefronts and rooming houses, shoddy apartment buildings, Model-T cars driving down the street, extras walking around. To fit in, Kirk and Spock steal some clothes hanging out to dry, which miraculously seem to fit them both perfectly.[1] To hide his ears, Spock puts on a beanie cap, pulled down.

This brings up some questions of ethics in time travel and changing the timeline. Kirk and Spock evidently have no moral qualms about petty theft when it comes to survival and a mission. What if the clothes they appropriated were someone's only possessions, were needed for work? What if a wife had washed and dried them, what is she going to tell her husband when the clothes are not to be found? Also, Spock uses the famous Vulcan "nerve pinch" to knock out a police officer who has caught them pilfering; he does this in front of half a dozen witnesses. These seemingly insignificant incidents could, in theory, alter the timeline in some way, just as McCoy's actions apparently have. Does the Prime Directive include no interference of the history of one's own society? A homeless man steals McCoy's phaser, thinking it valuable, and winds up pressing the overload button, vaporizing himself into oblivion. This death is never an issue; whether the man lived or died has no bearing on the overall timeline, showing that he is as expendable; he is a Depression bum who had no impact on humanity's fate.

Edith Keeler *does* have impact: a social activist running the 21st Street Mission, basically a soup kitchen (and possibly shelter) for men; it is never clear, but she is a "sister," either a nun or with the Salvation Army. She seems to run the kitchen by herself, hiring a few part-time employees. Kirk and Spock cross paths with her when they hide from the police in the dusty, dark basement of the soup kitchen. Keeler finds them and then hires them to clean up the basement; Kirk and Spock do such a fine, military-style mopping and cleaning that she hires them onto the kitchen and helps them rent a room in a boarding house, "a flop," at two dollars a week

Edith Keeler was played by Joan Collins, best known as the power hungry cougar from *Falcon Crest* and sister of bestselling author Jackie Collins. Collins' Keeler is optimistic, tough, alluring and vulnerable at the same time. She pontificates, through sermons, about a brighter, better future where man will "harness the energies of the atom" and explore the stars in "spaceships." She deals with men down on their luck that view her as a potential sex object, and this upsets Kirk. The attraction between Kirk and Keeler is immediate, and we know right off the two are destined to fall in love, for at the core of Ellison's story is a tragic romance of Shakespearean proportions—star-crossed intimates, soul mates who meet briefly across time but are doomed to never be together. Using his tri-corder like a proto search engine, Spock finds news articles of two separate histories—one where Keeler's reputation as a "slum area angel" wins President Roosevelt's attention, where her influence and pacifist movement keeps the United States out of World War II. This results in Nazi Germany's conquest of the world, the nexus of alteration in world history and the future of Starfleet. The other time-line reveals a headline "Social Worker Killed," a news item stating Keeler dies. Kirk and Spock realize McCoy somehow prevented her death, or perhaps he killed her in his cordrazine madness; either way, she is the "focal point" of two timelines and McCoy the "random element." Understanding that "Edith Keeler[2] must die," Kirk con-fronts the fact that he has fallen in love with the doomed woman; the crises of choice looms heavily over him.

Kirk spends quality time with Sister Keeler, justifying this as waiting for McCoy to cross paths with her. In one instance, he stops her from tripping and falling down the stairs, which could have killed her; Spock points out that may have been a serious error, that Kirk may have altered the timeline right then, rather than McCoy. Keeler is not drawn to Kirk sexually, as most of the women in the series are, but mentally and spiritually. The tragedy of his future broken heart is his own fault. His agency is self-inflicted pain, revealing that the macho Captain Kirk is not the flawless galactic hero he likes to present himself in the twenty-third century.

McCoy finally shows up and wanders into the soup kitchen, where Keeler helps him. Kirk runs across the street to the mission, just as McCoy walks out the door and Spock comes from a different direction. Keeler walks across the street. A truck is speeding her way, which she does not see. Kirk is about to save her from the truck and Spock admonishes him not to. Keeler is hit by the truck and killed on impact. McCoy is flabbergasted, Kirk devastated. McCoy asks, "Do you know what you've just done?" and Spock replies, "He knows, Doctor, he knows," as we hold on a haunted, harrowed Kirk who has just witnessed the death of his soul mate.

The three men are returned to the Time Planet, the *Enterprise* back in orbit and reality. Everyone is relieved that things have been set "right" except Kirk. He says, "Let's get the hell out of here," which, as noted earlier, was the first time in television history a swear word was broadcast.

The episode has plot issues. For a crew being on an exploratory mission, they depart from the planet and the Guardian of Time rather fast, without doing any further scientific investigation; something Spock, in character, would demand—although after being in 1930s New York for a long period, perhaps he is eager to get back to his quarters for some rest. We are not, however, told what the Guardian of Time truly is, who created it, who lived on this planet, why is the city in ruins.[3] Perhaps the obvious needs to be left a mystery; with all TV drama formats, only so much can be fit into forty-five minutes.

"EDITH KEELER MUST DIE"

Edith Keeler is not the usual run-of-the-mill female guest character; she does not show flesh and breasts and legs, she does not wear skimpy clothing, and she is not a promiscuous interstellar femme fatal. Sister Keeler is a spiritual woman haunted by visions of Utopia. Despite her gritty duties of dealing with the destitute, the homeless, and the alcoholics of the Depression, she is naïve when it comes to relationships with men as "beau," so she calls Kirk. Albeit her strength and independence, she easily succumbs to Kirk's charms; for love, she pays the ultimate price: death. It is fair to ask, "Why *does* Edith Keeler have to die?" Why doesn't McCoy or Kirk have to die, why wasn't it something they did (or did not do) that altered the future timeline? Why is the fate of the universe contingent on a woman's actions and demise, and not a man's? These same ethical, moral, and gendered questions have been applied to a "golden age" (1940s-1950s) science-fiction story, Tom Godwin's "The Cold Equations," first published in *Astounding Magazine* in 1954. A space ship makes the rounds of Earth's colonies, on a tight schedule from which it cannot deviate. Six people become infected with fatal virus and are dying from fever on a colony planet. The main ship drops off an "emergency dispatch" vessel of limited range, piloted by a man who has the serum that will cure the colonists. The pilot discovers there is a stowaway on board, eighteen-year-old Marilyn. She wants to see her brother, a colonist on the planet. The girl thinks that all she will have to pay a fine for her minor crime, but she winds up facing death. The ship only has enough fuel for the pilot and his cargo; her additional mass will cause the ship to run out of fuel before it can land, dooming not only herself and the pilot but the dying colonists below. The pilot attempts to find a solution; there is no way around what is dubbed "the cold equations." The best he can do is to alter the ship's course enough to give the girl a single hour's delay, before she must be jettisoned out into space. In that final hour, she writes letters to her parents and her brother, talks with the pilot about death and, in the last few minutes, is able to speak with her brother on the radio, allowing them to say their goodbyes. Marilyn enters the airlock and ejected into space. The story becomes a moral implication—the pilot needs to survive, needs to get the medication to the colonists, and needs to return to the mother ship. It is not his fault the girl made an error in judgment and put their lives in jeopardy, and there is no reason for him to sacrifice himself because she cannot pilot the craft, land it, and administer the antidote. Out of the love and concern for her brother, the girl dies for what she believes is an innocent act of breaking protocol. Her need for familial connection deprives her brother of ever seeing his sister again, deprives her parents of a child; it can be argued that Marilyn's youthful hubris was selfish and the nexus of her downfall.

"The Cold Equations" has been adapted for television three times: as part of the 1962 British anthology series *Out of This World*; as part of the 1985-89 revival of *The Twilight Zone*; and again in 1996 as a made-for-TV movie on the Sci-Fi Channel. Throughout the decades, the premise has been criticized for (1) possibly being scientifically and logically incorrect (any ship engineer would make sure there was reserve fuel in case of such emergencies; Don Sakers' 1991 short story "The Cold Solution" debunks the premise, and received the 1992 *Analog* Analytical Laboratory Award) and (2) a sexist view, portraying a woman's necessity to die at the hands of a man, for "the good" of all.[4] Is Edith Keeler's sacrifice fair?—because of her life and her political and social concerns, she has to die for doing good social work? It does not seem fair at all; she has become caught up in a problem that was not her doing. An event in the future—McCoy's accidentally overdosing on a drug—ripples backwards in time, and a saving of a life destroys millions of intended lives. Another question arises: if Edith Keeler knew the truth, if Kirk and Spock could explain it to her and she accepted this truth, would she elect to die, or would she have re-sisted fate and demanded her life?

These considerations change between the aired episode and the original script; deeper levels of meaning are presented, and we get to know more about Keeler's life and feelings, so that her death has a more devastating impact.

ELLISON'S SCRIPT

A crewmember moonlights as a drug dealer aboard the *Enterprise*. The drug pusher, Richard Beckwith, intentionally causes humans and aliens to become addicted to a "dream narcotic" called the Jewels of Sound. His agenda: turn the aliens they meet on the *Enterprise* voyages into cosmic junkies and steal whatever is valuable from them, or force them to give over all their wealth for a "fix." Saving the ill-gained currency, he wants to escape service in Starfleet and live the good life on an exotic planet, rich and comfortable. One of the bridge crew, Lieutenant LeBeque, finds himself addicted to the Jewels of Sound. Ellison describes the drug's effect through LeBeque's eyes:

> ...[his] face begins to simmer with weird lights, like a Van deGraaf generator, like heat-lightning off a rain-slick pavement. We HEAR the incredible MU-SIC OF JEWELS as they reach through LeBeque's head: part electronics, part orchestral and something like a scream from a creature dying horribly. Every-

thing GOES OUT OF FOCUS and the LIGHTS collide and merge and swirl and dance in patterns of no-pattern, and for SEVERAL BEATS, we SEE THRU the drug-drunken eyes of a man in the grip of an alien narcotic (*Plays* 21-22).

LeBeque finds himself as the helm of the *Enterprise* and nearly causes an accident. He is coming down from the drug and has no idea how he got there, where the hours have gone. LeBeque realizes that his drug problem is putting other lives, and the ship, in danger. He decides that he must find a way to quit. To make sure his dealer causes no more harm, he plans to turn Beckwith in. In a heated argument, Beckwith murders LeBeque and eludes capture by, like McCoy does, beaming down to the planet below. From the start, there were issues with this storyline. Ellison writes:

> I was advised by NBC network continuity [...] that drugs—even something as clearly as a fantasy construct as the Jewels of Sound—could not be permitted on a show that was airing so early in the evening. Further, there is a killing on board [...] I was told that was nixed because no one on board the starship *Enterprise* could be a bad guy. I railed against that concept. It always stuck me as nonsense that the network could try to pass off a space battle-cruiser of that size, with a complement of many hundreds of people,

without a few rotten apples in the barrel. Just the rigors of space, exploration and the tight confinement should have made *some*body go bananas. But, no, they didn't want to shatter the silly myth that all TV heroes are just that: heroes. (*Plays* 11)

Instead of an illegal drug, a medically approved pharmaceutical stimulant was replaced as a catalyst to get someone down to the planet and the time portal.

Beckwith changes history but the *Enterprise* does not vanish; it is replaced with a similar ship called the *Condor*, run by a "renegade" captain and his savage crew, who are just as perplexed as Kirk and company when the landing party beams up.[5] Ellison's time portal is not an entity itself; there are three Guardians that are

old, terribly old, as old as time itself, as old as the dying sun overhead. Nine feet tall, gray-silver in tone, shapeless beneath the long white robes that reach the mist-laden ground. They seem incredibly tall, not merely because they are a motionless nine feet in height, but because of their hair which rises up like mitered headpieces, because of the beards that hang down their silent faces [...] there is a vast dignity, an immense holiness about them (33-34).

The "ancients," the race that once inhabited the planet, have gone back in time of their own history, escaping the dying sun.[6] Kirk and Spock head back to earth catch Beckwith. The Guardians inform them that they will be drawn to the "focal point," the nexus, the reason why time was changed: "Blue it will be. Blue as the sky of Old Earth and clear as truth. And the sun will burn on it, and there is the key" (61). The "key," of course, is *Edith Keeler*. Spock realizes her lacuna when he sees her preaching with a blue placard behind her, and the sun glaring on it.

There is a major divergence in the interaction with Sister Keeler from the aired episode, and the theory of her role in history's alteration. Spock does not have his tricorder and he can only speculate what role Keeler plays—the United States staying out of the war and Germany developing the A-bomb is one (logical) scenario Spock posits. Kirk reveals a vulnerability to Spock that is against the grain of the canonical character: he says, "I've been on the move since I was old enough to ship on as a wiper in one of the old chemical-fuel rockets" (97). This cannot be true in *Star Trek* mythology; Kirk, an Iowa farm boy with stars in his eyes, was in Starfleet at an early age and previously served on the *U.S.S. Farragut,* revealed in the episode "Obsession" (12/16/67); further, "chemical-fuel" rockets are not used in Kirk's lifetime; warp drive was invented in the twenty-first century.

Keeler slips on the stairs and Kirk does not grab her, as he does in the aired version, but lets her fall, in case she is supposed to die that way. She knows he could have caught her and this confuses her, hurts her—this is the man she loves, and he allowed her injury; this does not make sense. Unlike the aired episode, Kirk considers allowing the alteration in history to stay as is, so she can exist and he can be with her. He considers remaining in the twentieth century and staying with her; he even desires to take her "back to the future" where she can live on the *Enterprise.*

Kirk faces two choices: the universe or love. "In the end," Ellison writes, "he would allow time to be warped and never returned to its original state" (*Plays* 13). Ellison was told by NBC and Roddenberry: "Our character would never act like that" (13), yet in the aired episode, it seems that Kirk does, briefly, consider doing this, but quickly gains his senses and returns to proper character.

When Beckwith moves to save Keeler from the oncoming truck, Kirk freezes and is unable to act. Spock stops Beckwith from changing time. In this moment of truth, Kirk has not made up his mind between love and history, because he neither stopped Beckwith nor saved Keeler; he stood dumbfounded, helpless, and watched. The script ends with Kirk in his quarters, suffering from loss. Spock understands Kirk's pain and moral dilemma, stating: "No woman was ever offered the universe for love" (137).

ARTISTIC AND PRAGMATIC DIFFERENCES

The evolution of "City" caused contention in Ellison and Roddenberry's friendship, each claiming bragging rights for its success. The script had been revised by a staff member, but it was not workable and upset Ellison—he so believed in his story that he did a rewrite for no pay. David Gerrold quotes Ellison:

> They put me in the backroom where the clothing de-
> signer [...] kept spare costumes, there was a table
> back there, and I wrote on that script—rewrote, be-
> cause they said they had to shoot it fast—I did four
> solid days' work, night and day, I slept on the floor in
> that back office, and wrote. In fact, the guards at De-
> silu used to come in at two in the morning with their
> guns drawn, they didn't know who the hell was in
> there, and they would see me sitting there with my
> eyes like a couple of poached eggs and they'd think,
> 'Oh, it's just the kook again with the story' (*World of
> Star Trek* 155).

Ellison still allowed his name on the credits, some-thing he has been known not to do when his scripts are al-tered, using the pseudonym "Cordwainer Bird" (as in "flipping the bird") instead. Either way, the episode was a hit with fans. The original script won the 1967-68 Writer's Guild of America's Best Teleplay for a dramatic series. Ellison notes in his introduction in *Plays*:

> "Star Trek" fans swear by the aired version, awarded
> it a Hugo at the World SF Convention, and a George

Méliès Fantasy award at the International Film Festival in 1973. I like to think the latter awards were given because that which I bled into the script could not be totally drained off. (9)

Roddenberry deemed his version superior, so much that the allotted $191,000 budget was upped to $262,000 "to make an episode they could all be proud of" according to Gerrold, adding: "Whether or not [Roddenberry's] rewrite was the best possible story is neither here nor there, art can never be independent of the context in which it is presented" (156), pointing out that at the end of the day, it was Roddenberry's show: his characters, his series, his authority: "The buck stopped at his desk" (156).

Some elements of Ellison's original script were taken out due to budget concerns, such as the three Guardians of Time: humanoid, nine-foot tall, statuesque and grand, rather than a single talking portal. Ellison's describes period New York City in quantitative detail, with more locations than what appear (and was feasible) in the episode. Introducing an alternate reality crew, the *Enterprise* changed to the *Condor,* would have required hiring more actors, having a separate set of costumes, and building a new set for the altered ship (and perhaps a new model of the *Condor* just to "see" how the ship of different). More often then not, a producer or director rewrites, changes, or deletes from a script, it is not an intentional alteration of a writer's vision out of ego but simply pragmatic choice. For instance, the episode suffers from a short romance between Kirk and Keeler; we never truly watch the evolution of their love deeply develop, to better understand why Kirk would be willing to sacrifice the universe for her. That development is present in the script; Ellison shows the little things, the tender moments, between Kirk and Keeler, and expands on their conversations and their compatibility.

ADAPTATION

Adaptation theory suggests that the visual product (film, TV, play) based on a literary work or pre-existing text—even the screenplay and teleplay—is a completely different work that needs not remain true to the original work. Studies in the adaptation of Charles Dickens' novels or William Shakespeare's plays point out how the films deviate greatly from the author's original vision and become the vision of screenwriters, directors, producers, and actors. In "Twelve Fallacies of Contemporary Adaptation Theory," Thomas Leitch notes "that movies are a collaborative medium, but is adaptation similarly collaborative, or is it the work of a single agent?" (149) Certainly, when Alfred Hitchcock adapted a pre-existing text, the product's author was more Hitchcock than the writer of the adapted source. In the case of "City," Roddenberry's adaptation of Ellison's teleplay is Roddenberry's vision of the story, influenced by the constraints of production mechanics: the four-act structure in forty-five minutes. The Kirk in Ellison's script is not the Kirk in Roddenberry's universe, and only two lines of dialogue from Ellison made it on screen, both spoken by the Guardian of Time: "Since before your sun burned hot in space, since before your race was born" and "Time has resumed its shape." The concept of the Guardian, the implications of time travel, and the character Edith Keeler are the authorial creations of Ellison, adapted to fit Roddenberry's needs. On March 13, 2009, Ellison filed a lawsuit against Paramount for twenty-five percent of all proceeds that have derived from "City": syndication fees, merchandise, the animated episode, the books, and any other storylines that originate from his concepts. Ellison contends he is due a percentage of any licensing proceeds from further adaptations of his characters and concepts.[7]

A third adaptation exits: James Blish's seventeen-page short story version in *Star Trek 2* (1968), a series where Blish condensed half a dozen episodes into a single book (fans refer to these as apocryphal stories). Blish took what he felt were the best elements of Ellison's script and Roddenberry's adaptation and created a new text. Sometimes, Blish inserted his own dialogue outside televised or teleplay versions; with "City," he changed Ellison, having Spock state at the end, "No other woman was ever offered the universe for love" to "no other woman was ever *almost* offered the universe for love."

CONCLUSION

The changes made from Harlan Ellison's original teleplay to the adapted, aired version on television is not a unique story, it has received more press and attention because of Ellison's status as a writer, fan reaction, and the awards both versions have won. Such alterations from script to screen are common in the television business; the difference between today's practice and the 1960s is that networks now hire a writing staff for each series rather than buying freelance script[8]—changes from an original draft are often made by the entire staff and during meetings, with the writer there, rather than behind closed doors, keeping the freelancer in the dark of the process until a finished revision is presented. The question of creative rights are more defined: a staff writer is an employee who punches a timecard; everything created in the writer's room, on the premises of the network lot, is the property of the network, so staff writers cannot make the claims Ellison has about ownership and license. The final authority, the ultimate writer of any episode, is the network.

COMMERCIAL BREAK: NOTES

1. In Ellison's original script, he wrote in the directions a plea to not use perfect-fitting clothes, but to have the clothes be too big or small, as that would be realistic. The clothes happen to be perfect fits for Kirk and Spock in the episode.

2. Keel over? Kill her? "He killed her"?

3. In the animated series, the novels, and *The Next Generation*, we learn the planet is placed under quarantine, designated top secret, supposedly used by historians only—although in *Voyager* and *Enterprise,* there exists a twenty-ninth-century "time police" branch of the Federation, who have used technology appropriated from the time planet to build time ships and are tasked with correcting changes in timelines, and enforce futures rules against time travel, imposing this policy on people from the past who are unaware of such laws. Obviously, having access to a time portal to any planet in the universe, with the power to change and influence both the past and the future, would be a mighty tool and weapon for unscrupulous factions with an agenda.

4. This is similar to the rhetorical logic in *Star Trek II: The Wrath of Kahn*: "The good of the many outweigh the good of the few, or the one."

5. This alternate reality concept, with an opposite, evil version of the Federation, was later borrowed in the episode "Mirror, Mirror."

6. This concept is the basis for "All Our Yesterdays" (3/14/69); it seems Ellison's first draft was material for three shows.

7. From the press release issued by Ellison's attorney notes that "the 1960 collective bargaining agreement between the WGA and the Producers, as amended in 1966, assures to the writers of individual teleplays 'a piece of the pie.' Specifically [...] Writers under that WGA agreement are supposed to get 25% of the revenue from the licensing of publication rights. From

Dollar One. Here, Paramount licensed its sister-corporation Simon & Schuster, through its Pocket Books division, the right to publish a knock-off trilogy of paperbacks—the 'Crucible' series—novels based on *City*, using Ellison's unique elements: plot, specific non-*Trek* characters, prominently including *The Guardian of Forever*, singular conceptual uses of time travel, the sense of tragedy that propels the story, the mood and venue of the story in the 1930s Great Depression, and at the stories' heart, pivotally, whether Edith Keeler lives or dies. Not merely minor points or window dressing or name-changes. No, they are the body, heart, and guts of Mr. Ellison's original creation—the best story *Star Trek* ever told." The release goes on. For more, see:

http://harlanellison.com/heboard/visitors/startrekpressrelease.html

8. The WGA, however, requires that each show buy three freelance scripts per season—while shows may buy these scripts, that does not necessarily mean they will produce and air them.

ACT IV

WAR, POLICY, AND LIFE AFTER CANCELLATION

COLD WAR IN SPACE

S tarfleet's foreign policy, desire for galactic expansion, conflict with the Klingons, Romulans, Gorn, and Tholians, and its rules of military engagement come to light in a number of episodes that have little to do with peaceful exploration and seeking out "new life and new civilizations." The decisions of starship captains result in policy change and the death of others; violence and paranoia overshadows rationale thought and diplomacy.

The *Enterprise*'s mission in "Errand of Mercy" (3/23/67) is "denying Organia to the Klingons," Kirk says to Spock, after a "Code One" message is sent from the Federation that diplomatic negotiations have broken down and war has been declared between the two factions over galactic territorial rights. The planet Organia has strategic positioning for war. The seemingly primitive and passive

Organians graciously turn down Kirk's impassioned plea that "in addition to military aid, we can send you specialists, technicians [...]We can help you build schools, educate the young." For all this, Kirk claims, "All we ask in return is that you let us help you." Kirk's rhetoric reflects Cold War American foreign policy in Korea, Vietnam, Cambodia, and elsewhere, extolling the virtues of capitalist democracy and the evils of Communist ideology. Kirk's description of his enemy certainly sounds like the black-and -white, good vs. evil portrayal of the Soviet Union: "The Klingons are a military dictatorship, war is their way of life." Kirk appears less concerned with the Organians' welfare, more over the planet's use by the Klingons as a base to launch attacks. Disguised as villagers, Kirk and Spock sabotage the Klingon outpost and murder Klingons with impunity, illustrating Kirk's statement earlier in the episode: "I'm a soldier, not a diplomat." The hubris of humans, Vulcans, and Klingons alike results in embarrassment; they have the tables turned on them: the Organians are not as simple as they appear and can re-shape reality by mere thought, "pure energy" beings who take on humanoid form only to interact with organic life, as Spock puts it, "for conventional points of reference."[1] They strip both sides of their military might and force the two factions into a treaty; although they have their own Prime Directive beliefs on non-interference with other life forms, they justify their actions as necessary to prevent a war that will results in the death of billions. The implications of the treaty are the root of further episodes where the Federation and Klingons vie for planets and civilizations.

In "The Trouble with Tribbles" (12/29/67), Space Station K-9 has a large stockpile of a new hybrid grain, "quadro-triticale," that will solve Sherman Planet's agricultural woes and sway the planet's government to join the Federation of Planets rather than the Klingon Empire. The *Enterprise* receives a "Priority One" emergency call; Kirk's assumes the Klingons have attacked since Priority One means "near or total disaster." Federation Under-Secretary of Agricultural Development Nils Baris authorized the call because he feels the Klingons will do something to sabotage the silos of quadro-triticale. This does not sit well with Kirk; he is irate and as far as the captain is concerned, the grain has little value in the bigger picture.

Baris is an uptight, dreary suit whose only concern is the success of his mission; he has a need to prove his command power over Kirk and the *Enterprise*, that he views are military tools for his means. The station manager, Mr. Lurry, is an exhausted man pushed around by politicians. Baris' assistant, Arne Darvin, appears to be another diplomat, but is a Klingon spy who has had his body surgically altered to look human.[2] The pivotal character Cyrano Jones, a small time asteroid miner and entrepreneur, has several small furry creatures he calls "tribbles" that he wants to sell as pets through the station's bar. He apparently has not had his tribbles for long because they prove to reproduce at an exponential rate. They are without gender and do not need a mate to gestate litters. McCoy examines the tribbles and all he can determine is that "almost fifty percent of the creature's metabolism is geared to reproduction." The more the tribbles eat, the bigger they get and more litters are produced. The tribbles wander into the quadro-triticale silos, consume all the grain, and gorge themselves to death in the process of their feeding frenzy. McCoy discovers the grain has been infected with a virus that clogs up the digestive system so beings are unable to break down and process the nutrients, "starving to death" even with all that food. The tribbles inadvertently become the saviors of Sherman's Planet and expose, through their deaths, the diabolical plot by the Klingons. With the conspiracy exposed, the Klingons are forced to leave, knowing they have lost Sherman's Planet to the Federation.

As comedy, "The Trouble with Tribbles" stands out from other episodes in its divergence from the characterization and approach. Some of the characters do not act or speak as they normally do, as the viewer has come to know them. Kirk appears disinterested in Starfleet's stake in Sherman's Planet, which goes against his role as an officer and his feelings in "Errand of Mercy." He is irritable, makes hasty decisions. He rapidly repeats words twice, a speech inflection not present in any other episode. Perhaps this has to due with "the pills" he gets from McCoy for the "headaches" he has been suffering. In the bar, Scotty, Chekov, and other crew members get drunk and have a bar brawl with the Klingons. The penultimate absurd scene, a common and popular promotional still for the series, is Kirk trapped neck-deep in dead and dying tribbles ("fat and sassy and lethargic" is how Gerrold describes them in the script [*Trouble with Tribbles* 228]) when he opens an overhead bin of the quadro-triticale and thousands of the creatures rain down. He does not jump out of the way but stands immobile with an exasperated expression.[2] The dead tribbles lead to the Klingon spy and a nefarious plot to discredit the Federation through mass homicide. In the chronology of the cold war, the Federation wins this round.

Kirk and crew clash with the Klingons in the battle for the hearts and minds of the natives in "A Private War" and "Friday's Child" (12/1/67), where each faction meets with community leaders and offer technology, weapons, and urban renewal. In each case, Kirk and crew defeat the Klingons intellectually and militarily, emphasizing good's triumph over evil, or America's superiority over Russia.

MOBY-DICK IN SPACE

In "The Doomsday Machine" (10/20/67) a distress call from the *U.S.S. Constellation* sends the *Enterprise* on a rescue mission, discovering a solar system scattered with debris; there were once several planets there but they no longer exist. The *Constellation* is badly damaged from a battle, hanging motionless in space, the crew mysterious missing. Kirk leaves Spock in command as he, Scotty, McCoy, and a couple of red shirts beam over to the empty ship.

One man has been left on board: Commodore Matt Decker, unshaven, exhausted from little sleep, half-mad with guilt and fear, claiming his ship was attacked by "that thing" but cannot explain further, as he freezes in a silent scream, remembering—the crew beamed down to a habitable planet for safety. Decker stayed behind. When Kirk states that there is no planet, Decker cries, "Don't you think I know that?! There was, but not anymore! They called me, they begged me for help, four hundred of them—I couldn't—I couldn't—" The transporter broke down and Decker could not beam his crew back up before the planet was destroyed and devoured.

The "thing" is an enormous planet-killing machine, "miles long," Decker says, shaped like a bent cone, with a gaping maw that emits a destructive anti-proton energy beam capable to blowing a planet into chunks; it then consumes the pieces for fuel. Spock theorizes that it is "essentially a robot; an automated weapon of immense size and power." Spock determines, via its path of eaten planets, that it originated outside the Galaxy and is headed for "the most densely populated" sectors of Federation space.

"They say there's no Devil, Jim," Decker tells Kirk, "but there is, right out of Hell, I saw it." This line of dialogue establishes Decker's role as Ahab in this episode's recognition of one American literature's greatest symbolic novels about man and God, *Moby-Dick* (1851/1977). Decker's mad rants about the machine, the devil, and what it did mirror Ahab's monologue about the white whale: "…it was Moby-Dick that dismantled me; Moby-Dick that brought me this dead stump I stand on now […] it was that accursed white whale that razed me; made a poor pegging lobber of me […] I'll chase him round Good Hope, and round the Horn […] and round perdition's flames before I give him up" (173). Decker's white whale, this doomsday device, is to him what Moby-Dick is to Ahab: a representation of failure, a force greater than man and man's need to conquer it. It is Moby-Dick in space.

To Kirk, it is just another alien technology that he has to deal with. Kirk posits that an ancient race, at war, built this machine; he delivers his characteristic philosophical monologue, alluding to the twentieth century:

> …did you ever hear of the Doomsday Machine? It's a weapon built primarily as a bluff; it was never meant to be used, so strong it could destroy both sides in war, something like the old H-Bomb was supposed to be. That's what I think this is. A Doomsday Machine that somebody used in a war uncounted years ago.

The glowing white, silver, and blue monstrosity aims its attention on the *Enterprise*. Kirk, trapped on the *Constellation* after the *Enterprise* is attacked, has no idea what has happened: Commodore Decker assumes command of the *Enterprise* and there is nothing Spock can do as regulations allow Decker, the commanding officer, to take control. What Decker truly wants is to fight the Doomsday Machine again, for personal, not military, reasons. Despite knowing their weapons are not effective, and that he lost his own ship trying to fight it, Decker puts the *Enterprise* and her crew in harm's way out his desire for revenge, just as Ahab endangers the men on the *Pequod* in his vengeful pursuit. The machine took Decker's crew, his confidence, and his identity as a commander. Decker, like Ahab, wants his leg back.

Decker, now suicidal, knowing he will never be able to live a sane life with all the death behind him, appropriates a shuttlecraft and flies it into the maw of the Doomsday Machine, blowing up his warp engines before being vaporized, hoping to cause an internal chain reaction that will destroy it. It is his final act of desperation, similar to Ahab's last spearing of Moby Dick; all that is missing is, "From Hell's heart I stab at thee."[3] Decker's act is not completely pointless; the shuttle's explosion did cause minimal damage and a drop in power. Kirk decides to fly the *Constellation* into the maw and cause greater damage.

Kirk's mettle is impressive at the end, having nearly lost his ship, witnessing the destruction of Federation property and life, and leaving behind a giant dead robotic weapon drifting in space; he strolls about the bridge with a cocky swagger and a smirk as he banters on the irony of what just happened: "Way back in the 20th Century, the H

Bomb was the ultimate weapon, their Doomsday Machine, and we used something like it to destroy another Doomsday Machine, probably the first time such a weapon was used for constructive purposes." The contemporary message is hardly subtle, similar to other episodes where Kirk outwits, outthinks, and out maneuvers machines and robots that have gone awry, from Nomad to the M-5 to Vaal the computer god: humanity trumps technology in the end. We must, again, put these morality plays in context of the era: computers were new, advancement in technology brought the nuclear age home, and fears that "machines will one day replacement humans" was commonly spoken of. Machines, however, break down, malfunction, go haywire: they are created by humans and thus, they cannot be greater than humans. Kirk proves this point over and over.

LIFE AFTER SEASON THREE

No series in television history has had the post-cancellation lifespan and expansion that *Star Trek* has enjoyed. It is now a corporate franchise, generating continued revenue for CBS-Paramount Television,[4] Bantam and Pocket Books, several comic book publishers,[5] network and cable providers, the actors, the estate of Gene Roddenberry, and the writers of the original novels.

The animated series aired two seasons in 1973-74 as a Saturday morning special. Most of the original cast returned to do the voices of their characters, except for Walter Koenig; there was not enough in the budget to add in Chekov, replaced by an alien navigator, Mr. Arexx, a being with three legs and three arms and minimal dialogue.[6] Animation allowed for elements not possible in a live action production: more outer space shots, exotic aliens that are large, made of rock or plants, that are aquatic or fly; action scenes set in space, deep under water, on ice planets; vast planetary-wide shots instead of the same simple set TOS used. The crew wore "life support belts" that covered them in an aura-like shield and allowed them to beam down to planets that did not have an atmosphere. The half-hour format called for fast-paced storylines. Themes and characters from TOS were re-visited: tribbles, the shore leave planet, Harry Mudd, and the Guardians of Time all return. The scripts were complex, well-written, maybe a little too intricate for children. NBC claimed the show was meant for the whole family to enjoy; however, the animated series was just as intricate in plot, storyline, and themes as TOS, dealing with issue of cloning, intergalactic holy war, land rights, personal rights, ethics of time travel, and the very nature of sentient consciousness. We see Kirk somewhat out of character, perhaps for the sake of young audiences: in "The Jihad" (1/12/74) a vivacious, statuesque female alien, Lara, expresses her attraction toward Kirk and makes several blatant (sexual) suggestions. Kirk passes and tells her, "Maybe some other time." In the live-action series, we know he would have acted on her proposal.

The animated series had the same issues as TOS with NBC over less-than-satisfactory ratings; it may have only lasted for one season but won a daytime Emmy, so was given a second season order. Eventually, Roddenberry decreed the animated series was not part of official canon; after his death, however, elements of the series were alluded to in other series episodes and the feature films, such as the use of Kirk's middle name, Tiberius, and the last name of Spock's mother, Amanda Grayson. Working within the half-hour format, the episodes had an uneven pacing; the voices often do not match the atmosphere of the scene: characters acting a bit too calm while in danger or running away alien beasts. This most likely had to do with the fact that the actors did not record their lines in real time, rehearsed, or together; in fact, Shatner recorded most of his while on the road, touring with a play, having only a script, a tape recorder, and no direction as to what was being animated. Alan Dean Foster adapted the series for Del Rey Books, titled *Star Trek Logs*.

James Blish wrote twelve volumes of *Star Trek* adaptations for Bantam Books; he died before completing the last one, co-written by his ex-wife, J. A. Lawrence. By the seventh volume, the stories started to become less truncated and more detailed; Blish would add in his own elements as would Foster in *Logs* (toward the final volumes, Foster fashioned entire novels out of a half-hour episode). The books were successful and the publishers realized there was a market for original *Star Trek* adventures. The first was penned by Blish, *Spock Must Die!* (1972), a short, 118-page novel; the premise is yet another trans-porter malfunction, where a duplicate Spock is created—only one could be allowed to live, *logically*, so the ethical and pragmatic dilemma was to determine which Spock was the "most real" and which was the copy. More novels followed, such as Kathleen Sky's *Vulcan!* (1975) and Joe Haldeman's *Planet of Judgment* (1978) set in what would have been seasons four or five of the five-year mission. Bantam released "photo novels" of TOS episodes; consist-ing of printed stills from selected shows, with dialogue balloons. This was long before a VCR was in every family home; the books allowed *Star Trek* fans to gaze on the im-ages of their heroes and re-live episodes.

When the license agreement with Bantam ran out, the book series went over to Pocket, an imprint of Simon and Schuster, owned by Gulf and Western, which owned Pa-ramount Studios. Pocket gradually stepped up the produc-tion of the occasional *Star Trek* novel to one a month; as the feature films and the new television shows earned new generations of fans, the novels became profitable com-modities and the books took on a life outside the movies and shows, although keeping within the franchise canon. Today, three-to-five *Star Trek* novels are published a month, in both hardback and mass market paperback, con-tinuing where the all the series have left off, mixing crew members together in cross-series storylines, and introduc-ing entire new characters and crews and ships. Multivolume story arcs have proven sustainable. Some books answer questions unanswered from the films and shows, such as the origin of the doomsday machine and the humpback whale probe in *The Voyage Home*. There are non-canonical books by William Shatner, where Kirk is resurrected from his death in *Star Trek: Generations* (1984) and Kirk goes on to have many more women and adventures in his new life.

FAN FICTION

In the early 1970s, two sub-genres emerged: fan and "slash" fiction. Fan fiction ("fanfic") is the amateur's take, without concern for canon, the market, good writing, or structured plot; fanfic could be a plotless day-in-the-life of, say, Mr. Spock, as he meditates in his quarters, or a poem written by Uhura. In fanfic, the writer can indulge in his or her fantasy with stories that would never be possible, such as explicit sexual encounters called "slash" that usually has to do with homosexual couplings—fans indulge in Kirk and Spock showing their "true love" for each other, perhaps adding in McCoy or Scotty for a threesome; or Mr. Sulu and Mr. Chekov meet up late at night, having suppressed their sexual longings all day while sitting next to each other at the helm. Slash has been critically examined in academia as a cultural oddity in pop culture; critics of sociology, psychology, mass media, and literature alike have examined and explicated slash texts, which are not limited to *Star Trek*; there is slash for nearly all successful genre television—*Buffy the Vampire Slayer*, *Battlestar Galactica*, *Miami Vice*, *The Sopranos*. Slash offers fans an avenue to explore sexual desires they project onto their favorite characters.

As video technology became cheaper and easier to use, it was inevitable that fans would start creating visual fanfic. The pioneer is *Star Trek: The New Voyages,* which continues the remaining years of the original five-year mission, disregarding canon. While amateur actors in costumes play Kirk, Spock, McCoy, Scotty, Sulu, Chekov, and Uhura (often in pastiche form, overemphasizing William Shatner's trademark characteristics, Spock's quirks, or Scotty's and Chekov's accents), the scripts have exhibited professional craftsmanship, written by fans that know the show well. The success of *New Voyages* is aided by the building of exact and detailed (and intentionally low-budget) replicas of the *Enterprise* bridge, sickbay, and other settings, including alien planets. With special effects technology accessible to those outside the usual tenants of the industry, the space ships in battle, transporter effects, and alien life forms are enhanced with CGI software. *New Voyages* has featured original actors: Walter Koenig appears as Chekov's grandfather and George Takei appears as Captain Sulu of the *U.S.S. Excelsior* in a multi-era storyline. D.C. Fontana, *Star Trek*'s original story editor who penned a number of episodes, contributed a script. CBS-Paramount has allowed these Internet episodes (which are structured in a four-act, teaser and coda format of a one-hour drama, even with commercials between the acts and the classic NBC logo and peacock at the beginning) to exist as long they are available to view for free and no one is making money; all writing, acting, production, and web hosting must be without fees or salaries paid.

The reason why CBS-Paramount allows *New Voyages* and the many other similar web-based shows, which now include more than a dozen, to broadcast is that these outlets create new fans, and new fans watch reruns, buy novels, and purchase merchandise. For CBS-Paramount, visual fanfics act as promotion and advertising that keeps the franchise financially healthy, a mutually beneficial situation for both sides, each getting something of value. There is also this to consider: *New Voyages* boasts having upward to forty million downloads of all episodes, whereas the series *Enterprise* started off with twelve million viewers and was cancelled when it had a mere two million (considered a failure in network broadcast numbers).

SPIN-OFFS

The most significant post-series elements are the eleven features films and four spin-off shows. Throughout the 1970s, Roddenberry worked to revive *Star Trek* on television, adding new characters to the crew; after many false starts and misdirection in development, elements of the pilot were transformed into *The Motion Picture. Star Wars* was successful by then and studios were seeking to fulfill the public's desire for more science fiction features. *The Wrath of Kahn, The Search for Spock*, and *Voyage Home* were all critical and financial successes, although *The Final Frontier* and *The Undiscovered Country* were not received with similar satisfaction by critics and fans.[7] *Generations* was a cross over of TOS and *Next Generation. First Contact* was a time travel story with the Borg in twenty-first-century Earth, and concerned humanity's first meeting with Vulcans.

The Next Generation, Deep Space Nine, and *Voyager* all lasted seven seasons and maintained satisfactory ratings; *Enterprise*, on the other hand, suffered from low ratings, budget cuts, and threats of cancellation, remaining on air in a fourth season with deep budget cuts reminiscent of the third season of TOS.[8] The feature films *Insurrection* and *Nemesis*, despite hype and the hiring of an Oscar-winning screenwriter for *Nemesis*, were not as critically and financially successful as the previous *Next Generation* movies. There were rumors among fans that a new series or film would feature the adventures of Captain Sulu and the *U.S.S. Excelsior*, but that did not develop. Sulu storylines were only to be found in novels, audio tapes, and video games—and plenty of fanfic.

A Revisionist *Star Trek*

In 2007, veteran television director J. J. Abrams (*Alias*, *Lost*) and his production team of writers and designers were hired to conceive and direct the eleventh feature, a prequel with new actors playing Kirk, Spock, McCoy, *et al.*, in younger form (Leonard Nimoy makes a cameo as the older Spock from another timeline). The movie was released on May 8, 2009, with a mixed reception among fans, yet was a commercial success at the box office, reviving the faltering franchise. Abrams intended the movie to attract a general audience—one need not be a fan or know canonical facts to watch it. Elements from the novels were also incorporated, such as an early relationship between Commander Spock and Corpsman Uhura, young Kirk's abusive uncle (the scenes were cut in the film's final version) and the possibility of multiple timelines and alternate histories. The film shows the characters as children: the thrill-seeking Iowa farm boy Kirk, always getting into trouble; Spock's inner turmoil with his human and Vulcan blood, and the social stigma from peers; McCoy's conflict with wanting to be a doctor and his issues with the military. The special effects and technology onboard the *Enterprise* (much like the *Enterprise* series) is digital and complex, rather than the push-button, analog, low tech in TOS. Canon changes in a number of significant ways: Captain Christopher Pike becomes wheelchair-bound after his torture at the hands of the Romulans rather than an accident from radiation poisoning in "The Menagerie," leading to Kirk's command as replacement. In this movie, a young Kirk takes command by circumstance and necessity, never having served on the U.S.S. Farragut, which makes several TOS episodes that connect to Kirk's early career obsolete, as well as "The Menagerie" and Spock's court-martial for "saving" his old Captain. The Kirk in the movie is an angry rebel, having grown up without a father, George Kirk, who died at the Romulans' hands on the U.S.S. Kelvin. In original canon, George Kirk lived to see his son take command of the Enterprise. These alterations are explained as the result of timelines changed by the Romulan villain, Nero, played by Eric Bana, whose desire for revenge against Spock and the Federation, and his ship's accidental trip back in time, leads him to destroy Vulcan and attack Earth, so Starfleet will never exist. Leonard Nimoy reprises his role as an elderly Spock, the only original actor make a cameo; Spock is the cause of the black hole that sends Nero's ship—and his own ship—back in time. William Shatner wanted to return as Kirk, but, in keeping to the canon of the films, Kirk has been dead since Generations, and producers refused to resurrect him. Paramount had ordered all novels dealing with TOS timelines to go on hiatus until the new movie came out; with these changes in history, the novels will now follow suit. The door has been opened for a whole new five years of revisionist adventures and additional films and perhaps another television series. The difference: the timelines now has two Spocks—one elderly, one young (again, the doppelgänger effect)—and Kirk has taken command of the *Enterprise* while still in his twenties, instead of age thirty-five in TOS, when he was still the youngest officer to be given a command. In the movie, Kirk never pays his dues through rank—in a matter of days, he goes from cadet to lieutenant to first officer to captain, a reward for saving Earth, the Federation, and destiny. With history changed, one wonders if the *Enterprise* will still have the same adventures as in TOS, and will Kirk never go back to New York in the 1930s and fall in love with Edith Keeler? Likewise, will they never fight The Doomsday Machine, leaving the weapon to make its way to Earth? Anything can happen when you have endless alternate universes to play with.

COMMERCIAL BREAK: NOTES

1. The Organians are similar to the omnipresent, god-like beings of the Q Continuum in *The Next Generation*, forcing their own policy on lesser, corporeal beings across the universe.
2. Just as the evolutionary process of Ellison's "City" from idea to script to episode is educational in the process of television production, "Tribbles" went through a series of treatments, outlines, and drafts; the creatures were originally called "the Fuzzies" (43) and looked like small teddy bears.

3. In *Star Trek II: The Wrath of Kahn*, Kahn utters these words before detonating the Genesis bomb, believing he has finally killed his own white whale who ruined his life: Admiral James T. Kirk.

4. CBS and Paramount merged January, 2006.

5. The license fee per TOS character is in the neighborhood of one million dollars.

6. Koenig wrote one of the episodes, "The Infinite Vulcan" (10/20/73), the first actor to pen a *Star Trek* adventure.

7. The fifth movie, directed by Shatner, is sometimes referred to by fans as *Star Trek V: Death of a Franchise*, as warmly noted in Shatner's Comedy Central roast.

8. *Enterprise*'s episodes often rehashed themes and ideas from previous series episodes (the mirror-mirror universe, the transporter or holodeck malfunction, and the dreaded superior alien being testing humanity). That is not to say *Enterprise* was not completely without merit and did not attempt to push the envelope at times; indeed, the *über*-story reflected present-day state of world politics the way the original series did: an unknown alien race commits a terrorist attack against earth, destroying all of Florida, and so the *Enterprise* is sent on a (possible suicide) mission to find out who these aliens are and why they want to destroy Earth; and to reach an agreement of peace or destroy the other race before it can engage in more terrorist attacks. The crew is split between seeking a dialogue and wanting revenge for the millions of people who died. Captain Archer and his crew discover is that there is a "temporal cold war" going on between the Federation in the twenty-seventh

century and a time-traveling race known as the Suliban who know they will be defeated by human beings one day, so in an effort to change that future timeline, they deceive another race into believing Earth will destroy their planet in the future, causing this race to make a pre-emotive strike long before the Federation can become a galactic super power. Overtones of 9/11, the war on terror, pre-emptive measures, and governments using other governments as war paws were all over this story arc. The themes of going back in time to change Earth's and the Federation's destiny was already explored in *Star Trek: First Contact* and several television episodes. However, just as Archer thinks he and his crew have saved the world, the *Enterprise* gets tossed back into time and an alternate universe, where the Suliban have joined forces with Nazi Germany and have control over the entire world; once again, it is up to an *Enterprise* captain to save the galaxy and restore the history of World War II as we all know it.

CODA/CREDIT WINDOW

Taking the post-structural contention that each individual derives his/her own meaning to a text outside the mainstream institutional "truth"—or "to each his own bauble" as Baudrillard stated (*Ecstasy of Communication*, 47)—*Star Trek* had, and still has, an influence on my life; from childhood to my teen years to early adulthood and now, here on the outskirts of middle-age (my personal city on the edge of forever), *Star Trek* has played a significant role in shaping who I am as a television viewer, a fan, a working writer, and a scholar.

I have discussed how *Star Trek* is television content that influenced reality and the Utopian society it is set in is not as perfect and equal as the propaganda would have it. Captain Kirk and his crew constantly violate the Prime Directive and the freedom and rights of alien races who never invited humans to come to their planets and force change in social, religious, and governmental structure, and Kirk does so without approval from the Federation or considering the long term consequences of his actions.

I set out to explore what makes *Star Trek* a milestone in television, and determine why such an iconic show was not successful when originally aired. One reason is logistical: when networks continuously move a series from one day and time slot to another, loss of viewership in inevitable; fans require consistency and often arrange their own schedules to make sure they are home on certain nights to watch a specific show, and a 8 P.M. timeslot often makes a world of difference to a 10 P.M. timeslot, especially for households that watch television during dinner or at bedtime. I will also suggest that the series was simply "before its time"; the social and political atmosphere in 1966-68 was too turbulent for an optimistic vision of the future where all ethnicities and races live and work in harmony. It was not until Vietnam and the counter-culture movement simmered down that *Star Trek* was ready to capture its international audience and millions of fans. Mankind had made it to the moon, thus science-fiction was now science-fact; the computer age was around the corner, the gadgets and technology represented a future that seemed possible.

The show has become ingrained into the communal psyche, spawning subcultures of fan(atic)s, tribes of the devoted, fictional languages used in every-day life, and a consumer religion, translated into profit and a continued manufacturing of new products. *Star Trek* possesses a staying power in the milieu of broadcast history unlike any other program, iconographic in the same manner that *The Honeymooners*, *I Love Lucy*, and *M*A*S*H** defined a time and atmosphere in history, to be examined a hundred years from now as visual artifacts of entertainment culture.

VIDEOGRAPHY

SEASON ONE

"The Man Trap." 8 September 1966

The *Enterprise* visits planet M-113 where scientist Dr. Crater and his wife Nancy, an old girlfriend of Dr. McCoy's, are studying the remains of an ancient civilization. Shortly after their arrival, crewmen start turning up dead, drained of salt, and left with unusual red marks on their faces.

"Charlie X." 15 September 1966

The spaceship *Antares* rescues Charles Evans from the surface of planet Thasus, and then quickly hands him off to the *Enterprise*. The teen reveals his psionic powers and desire for godhood.

"Where No Man Has Gone Before." 22 September 1966

The flight recorder of the 200-year-old *U.S.S. Valiant* reveals a magnetic storm at the edge of the galaxy.

"The Naked Time." 29 September 1966

The crew is infected with a mysterious disease that removes all emotional and social inhibitions.

"The Enemy Within." 6 October 1966

A transporter malfunction splits Captain Kirk into two people: one meek and indecisive, the other violent and irrational.

"Mudd's Women." 13 October 1966

The *Enterprise* picks up devious entrepreneur Harry Mudd; he is accompanied by three beautiful women who immediately put a spell on all the male crewmembers.

"What Are Little Girls Made Of?" 20 October 1966

Kirk and Nurse Chapel beam down to Exo III, to meet with her former fiancée, Roger Korby. Korby is protected by the ancient android, Ruk, and assisted by the beautiful Andrea, also and android.

"Miri." 27 October 1966
The *Enterprise* visits an Earth-duplicate planet that has been in ruins for 300 years, populated with children who have a disease that vastly slows the aging process.

"Dagger of the Mind." 3 November 1966
Kirk and psychiatrist Helen Noel are trapped on a maximum-security penal colony that experiments with mind control.

"The Corbomite Maneuver." 10 November 1966
The *Enterprise* is met by an extremely powerful ship that plans on destroying the *Enterprise* for trespassing. Kirk bluffs his way out of this destruction by the fallacious "Corbomite device."

"The Menagerie: Part 1." 17 November 1966
The *Enterprise* is hijacked by Spock, leaving Captain Kirk on a Starbase. Spock has also kidnapped Captain Christopher Pike, the ship's former commander, recently crippled by an accident. The destination: Talos IV, a planet off limits by Federation order since the *Enterprise* encountered it years ago, under Pike's command.

"The Menagerie: Part 2." 24 November 1966
Spock is court-martialed. We learn that Spock was acting on Pike's behalf; crippled in real life, on Talos IV, the Talosians place Pike in an imaginary world where he is

healthy, young, and in love with a beautiful human mate, Vina.

"The Conscience of the King." 8 December 1966
Kirk investigates whether an actor is actually an infamous mass murderer; someone is killing the witnessed who can identify him. Shades of the Holocaust and Nazi death camps is implied.

"Balance of Terror." 15 December 1966
A Romulan ship makes a destructively hostile armed probe of Federation territory. This is the first conflict between the Federation and the Romulan Empire.

"Shore Leave." 29 December 1966
An apparently uninhabited planet is run by a giant psychic computer that can manufacture whatever a person thinks of.

"The Galileo Seven." 5 January 1967
A shuttle under Spock's command crash-lands on a hostile planet.

"The Squire of Gothos." 12 January 1967
An eccentric superior being that controls matter and creates planets wants to "play" with the Enterprise crew. The being is actually a child.

"Arena." 19 January 1967

A lizard-like alien race known as the Gorn destroys an Earth colony. The *Enterprise* pursues the fleeing Gorn vessel until another race of powerful aliens intervene and force Captain Kirk and the Gorn captain to face off in one-on-one combat in which the winner will be released and the loser and his ship destroyed. Once again, humanity is tested by superior beings.

"Tomorrow Is Yesterday." 26 January 1967

The *Enterprise* is somehow thrown back in time to 1960s Earth and have to restore the timeline. They meet an alien time traveler who is tasked to stop events that could create an apocalypse in earth's future.

"Court Martial." 2 February 1967

Kirk is charged and court-martial with the negligent death of a crewman. Like "Turnabout Intruder," Kirk's early success as an officer causes jealousy in former friends.

"The Return of the Archons." 9 February 1967

The *Enterprise* goes to Beta 2 to investigate the fate of the *U.S.S. Archon*, missing for a century. They discover a society of seemingly peaceful people called "the Body" and controlled by a cult leader, Landru, a megalomaniac computer.

"Space Seed." 16 February 1967
The *Enterprise* finds a twentieth-century spaceship, the *Botany Bay*, that contains dozens of people in suspended animation, genetic "supermen" that escaped Earth after the Eugenics Wars of the 1990s.

"A Taste of Armageddon." 23 February 1967
Kirk and Spock must save their ship's crew when they are declared all killed in action in a strange computer-simulated war where those deemed virtually murdered must report to disintegration chambers.

"This Side of Paradise." 2 March 1967
The *Enterprise* is dispatched to Omicron Ceti III, believed to be under constant irradiation from deadly Berthold Rays, in order to evacuate the colonists. Upon arrival, however, it seems that the colonists are in perfect health and have no desire to leave.

"The Devil in the Dark." 9 March 1967
The *Enterprise* is sent to a mining colony that is being terrorized by a mysterious silicon-based creature, or living rock.

"Errand of Mercy." 23 March 1967
Organia, inhabited by simple pastoral folk, lies on a tactical corridor likely to be important in the coming conflict between the Federation and Klingon Empire. The Organi-

ans are actually powerful beings who force the two sides into a Peace Treaty.

"The Alternative Factor." 30 March 1967
Kirk, Spock and a security force beam down to a planet and find a man named Lazarus, locked in a struggle with another being composed of "anti-life."

"The City on the Edge of Forever." 6 April 1967
A temporarily maddened Dr. McCoy alters history and changes earth's past and future. Kirk and Spock follow him to 1930s New York to prevent it. The woman Kirk falls in love must die for time to be restored.

"Operation—Annihilate!" 13 April 1967
The *Enterprise* crew must stop a plague of flying parasites from possessing human bodies and spreading throughout the galaxy.

SEASON 2

"Amok Time." 15 September 1967
In the heat of a seven-year itch, the *Pon Farr* mating period, Spock must return to Vulcan to meet his intended future wife, betrothed from childhood.

"Who Mourns for Adonis?" 22 September 1967
A powerful being claiming to be the Greek god Apollo demands that the crew of the *Enterprise* worship him.

"The Changeling." 29 September 1967
A powerful artificial intelligence called Nomad thinks Kirk is its creator.

"Mirror, Mirror." 6 October 1967
During an ion storm, a transporter malfunction sends Kirk, McCoy, Scotty and Uhura into in a "mirror universe" aboard a parallel (alternative) *Enterprise* run by ruthless barbarians.

"The Apple." 13 October 1967
The *Enterprise* landing party finds a primitive village devoted to service and worship of a needy computer god called Vaal.

"The Doomsday Machine." 20 October 1967.
The *Enterprise* encounters the wrecked U.S.S. *Constellation* and its distressed captain, who is determined to stop the giant planet destroying robot ship that killed his crew.

"Catspaw." 27 October 1967
Kirk and Spock lead a party beaming down to a normally barren planet where a superior life form lures them by images of three witches, a cat, and a castle.

"I, Mudd." 3 November 1967
Harry Mudd returns with a plot to take over the *Enterprise* by stranding the crew on a planet populated by androids.

"Metamorphosis." 10 November 1967
The *Enterprise* encounters a mysterious energy cloud that pulls them down to planet Gamma Canaris N, where they meet a man claiming to be Zefram Cochrane, the inventor of the Warp Drive in the twenty-first century.

"Journey to Babel." 17 November 1967
The *Enterprise* hosts a number of quarrelling diplomats, including Spock's father, Sarek. A murder occurs.

"Friday's Child." 1 December 1967
The *Enterprise* is on a mission to a primitive, warlike planet to negotiate a supply contract for a vital mineral. They find a Klingon has already gained the inhabitants' trust.

"The Deadly Years." 8 December 1967
The landing party is exposed to strange forms of radiation that rapidly ages them.

"Obsession." 15 December 1967
Kirk obsessively hunts for a mysterious homicidal cloud creature he encountered as a Lieutenant on the *U.S.S. Farragut.*

"Wolf in the Fold." 22 December 1967
Scotty is accused of murdering women on a pleasure planet.

"The Trouble with Tribbles." 29 December 1967
Kirk is annoyed when he has to deal with Federation bureaucrats, self-righteous Klingons, and a peddler who sells furry, purring, hungry little creatures as pets.

"The Gamesters of Triskelion." 5 January 1968
Kirk, Uhura, and Chekov are trapped on a planet where gladiators are enslaved and trained to perform for the amusement of bored, bodiless aliens: colored brains in containers.

"A Piece of the Action." 12 January 1968
Aliens emulate a book about Chicago gangsters left by a Federation ship.

"The Immunity Syndrome." 19 January 1968
The *Enterprise* encounters a gigantic energy draining space organism that threatens to devour the galaxy.

"A Private Little War." 2 February 1968
Kirk returns to the planet Neural which he had spent time thirteen years before. A friend of his from his previous visit is now leader of his people.

"Return to Tomorrow." 9 February 1968
The last three members of an ancient disembodied race wish to borrow the bodies of Kirk, Spock, and Dr. Mulhall for pleasure and power.

"Patterns of Force." 16 February 1968
Looking for a missing Federation cultural anthropologist, Kirk and Spock find themselves on a planet modeled on the German Nazi Party.

"By Any Other Name." 23 February 1968
The *Enterprise* answers a distress cal. The landing party is told to surrender by Rojan, a psychic being who can control minds.

"The Omega Glory." 1 March 1968
Responding to a distress signal, Kirk finds Captain Tracey of the *U.SS. Exeter* violating the Prime Directive.

"The Ultimate Computer." 8 March 1968
Kirk is ordered to test out an advanced artificially intelligent control system that could potentially render command structure redundant.

"Bread and Circuses." 15 March 1968
While searching for the crew of a destroyed spaceship, the Enterprise discovers a planet whose oppressive government is a twentieth-century version of Earth's Roman empire.

"Assignment: Earth." 29 March 1968
The *Enterprise* is assigned to visit the twentieth century to study critical political tensions. After arriving, they intercept a transporter beam that originates at least a thousand light-years from Earth.

SEASON 3

"Spock's Brain." 20 September 1968
An unidentified female from an advanced civilization transports aboard the *Enterprise* and, after rendering the entire crew unconscious, removes Spock's brain.

"The *Enterprise* Incident." 27 September 1968
The *Enterprise* deliberately crosses the Neutral Zone, on Kirk's orders, into Romulan space and is promptly surrounded by Romulan warships, each equipped with a "cloaking device" that renders it undetectable. The mission is to steal the cloaking device.

"The Paradise Syndrome." 4 October 1968
Trapped on a planet whose inhabitants resemble American Indians, Kirk loses his memory and is proclaimed a god.

"And the Children Shall Lead." 11 October 1968
The *Enterprise* finds a Federation colony where the adults have all killed each other but the children, led by an alien entity, play without care.

"Is There in Truth No Beauty?" 18 October 1968
The *Enterprise* transports the Medusan Ambassador Kollos and his telepathic interpreter Dr. Miranda Jones. Humans go mad if they look at a Medusan. Only Vulcans can handle the horrible sight.

"Spectre of the Gun." 25 October 1968
As punishment for trespassing, aliens condemn Kirk and his landing party as the losing side of a simulation of the gunfight at the O.K. Corral. This is an experiment for the aliens to understand the human concept of right and wrong.

"Day of the Dove." 1 November 1968
A violent entity traps the *Enterprise* crew and the crew of a disabled Klingon ship.

"For the World Is Hollow and I Have Touched the Sky." 8 November 1968

The *Enterprise* discovers that an asteroid on a collision course with a planet is actually a generation ship.

"The Tholian Web." 15 November 1968

Kirk and the *U.S.S. Defiant* vanish into a spatial interphase between universes. They have trespassed into the Tholian Annex and the Tholians are not happy about it.

"Plato's Stepchildren." 22 November 1968

On an urgent medical emergency call, Kirk, Spock, and McCoy encounter an alien society who had once flourished on earth during the time of Plato.

"Wink of an Eye." 29 November 1968

The *Enterprise* is called to an advanced planet to help with an emergency. Beaming down, though, they can find no people, only cities. The people exist in speeded up time and want to hijack the *Enterprise*.

"The Empath." 6 December 1968

Trapped in an alien laboratory, Kirk, Spock, and McCoy meet an "empath" and are subject to a series of invasive experiments.

"Elaan of Troyius." 20 December 1968
The *Enterprise* transports Elaan, the female ruler of the warrior Troyians, to the planet of the enemy, so that her arranged marriage will halt their interplanetary war.

"Whom Gods Destroy." 3 January 1969
Kirk and Spock are taken prisoner by a former starship captain named Garth, who has taken over a high security asylum for the criminally insane.

"Let That Be Your Last Battlefield." 10 January 1969
The *Enterprise* encounters two duo-chromatic and mutually belligerent aliens who put the ship in the middle of their centuries-old conflict.

"The Mark of Gideon." 17 January 1969
Kirk beams down to the planet Gideon and finds himself trapped on a deserted replica of the *Enterprise*.

"That Which Survives." 24 January 1969
The landing party finds a deserted outpost guarded by the deadly image of a beautiful woman.

"The Lights of Zetar." 31 January 1969
The *Enterprise* is on course to install new equipment on Memory Alpha, the central library storage facility for the Federation. Scotty has been working closely on the project with Lieutenant Mira Romaine and falls in love with her.

"Requiem for Methuselah." 14 February 1969

Kirk, Spock, and McCoy beam down to a supposed uninhabited planet to gather the mineral ryetalyn to fight a plague of Rigelian fever on board the *Enterprise*.

"The Way to Eden." 21 February 1969

The *Enterprise* is ordered to pursue a group of anti-establishment idealists who have stolen a shuttlecraft to get to the mythical planet Eden.

"The Cloud Minders." 28 February 1969

Kirk and Spock are caught up in a revolution on a planet where intellectuals and artists live on a Utopian city in the sky while the rest of the population toils in mines on the barren surface below. The gases of the mines make the lower class people savage-like and dumb-witted.

"The Savage Curtain." 7 March 1969

Kirk, Spock, and Abraham Lincoln are pitted in battle against four notorious villains from history. The purpose is to help a molten rock creature understand the concept of good vs. evil.

"All Our Yesterdays." 14 March 1969

Kirk, Spock, and McCoy transport down to the planet Sarpeidon to investigate the planet's evacuation before its sun goes nova. The three wind up going into the planet's past. Spock falls in love.

"Turnabout Intruder." 3 June 1969

As revenge against Kirk for breaking her heart long ago, Dr. Janice Lester arranges for an alien machine to swap the consciousness of Kirk and herself so she can take command of the *Enterprise*. The airdate of this final episode of TOS was delayed due to the death of former President Eisenhower.

WORKS CITED

Andreadis, Athena. *To Seek Out New Life: The Biology of Star Trek.* NY: Crown, 1998.

Anon. "Klingon Speakers Now Outnumber Navajo Speakers." *The Onion* 29 July 1999, n.p.

Baker, Mitzi. "'Star Trek'-type scans may reveal tumor genetics." *Stanford Report* 23 May 2007, n.p.

Baudrillard, Jean. *Simulations.* NY: Semiotext(e), 1983.

——. *The System of Objects.* London: Verso, 1996.

Blair, Karin. *Meaning in Star Trek.* Chambersburg, PA: Anima Books, 1977.

——. "Sex and *Star Trek.*" *Science-Fiction Studies* 10.2 (Spring 1983): 292-297.

Blish, James. *Star Trek 2.* NY: Bantam, 1968.

——. *Spock Must Die!* NY: Bantam, 1970.

Blumer, Harold. *Symbolic Interactionism: Perspective and Method.* Chicago: University of Chicago Press, 1969.

Cova, Bernard, Robert Kozinets, and Avi Shankar. *Consumer Tribes*. Boston: Butterworth-Heinemann, 2007.

Cranny-Francis, Ann. "Sexuality and Sex-Role Stereotyping in *Star Trek*." *Science-Fiction Studies* 12.3 (Winter 1985): 274-284.

Crispin, A.C. *Yesterday's Son*. NY: Pocket, 1983.

Csicsery-Ronay, István, Jr. "Escaping *Star Trek*." *Science-Fiction Studies* 32.31 (November 2005): 503-511.

Denzin, Norman K. *Images of Postmodern Society: Social Theory and Contemporary Cinema*. Newbury Park: Sage Publications, 1991.

Ellison, Harlan. "'Repent, Harlequin!' said the Ticktockman." *Galaxy,* December 1965. rpt. in Ellison's *Paingod and Other Delusions*, NY: Pyramid Books, 1975.

——. "The City on the Edge of Forever." See Elwood.

——. *Harlan Ellison's The City on the Edge of Forever: The Original Teleplay That Became the Classic Star Trek® Episode*. Clarkson, GA: White Wolf Publishing, 1996.

Ellison, Harlan, ed. *Dangerous Visions*. NY: Doubleday, 1967.

Elwood, Roger, ed. *Six Science Fiction Plays.* NY: Pocket, 1975.

Gerrold, David. *The World of Star Trek.* NY: Ballantine, 1972.

——. *The Trouble with Tribbles*. NY: Ballantine, 1973.

Godwin, Tom. "The Cold Equations." *Astounding Magazine*. August, 1954.

Goodwin, Laura. "Sex and the *Star Trek* Woman." Accessed at http://allyourStar Trekarebelongto.us/ tos-sex.htm

Haldeman, Joe. *Planet of Judgment.* NY: Bantam, 1978.

Harrison, Taylor, Projansjy, Sarah, Ono, Kent A., and Elyce Rae Helford, eds. *Enterprise Zones: Critical Positions on* Star Trek. Boulder, CO: Westview Press, 1996.

Helford, Elyce Rae. "A Part of Myself No Man Should Ever See: Reading Captain Kirk's Multiple Masculinities." In *Enterprise Zones: Critical Positions on* Star Trek. Harrison, Taylor, Projansjy, Sarah, Ono, Kent A., and Elyce Rae Helford, eds. Boulder, CO: Westview Press, 1996.

Helman, Kate. "*Star Trek: The Original Series:* Season Three DVD Review." http://www.tvdvdreviews.com/ starStar Trek3.html

Hermans, Judith. "Klingon and Its Users: A Sociolinguistics Profile." M.A. thesis, Tilburg University, 1999. http://www.judion.de/klingon/

Kraemer, Ross S., Cassidy, William and Susan L. Schwartz. *Religions of Star Trek.* Boulder, CO: Westview Press, 2001.

Kozinets, Robert. V. "Utopian Enterprise: Articulating Meaning in *Star Trek's* Culture of Consumption." *Journal of Consumer Research*, Vol. 28, June 2001: 67-88.

Krauss, Lawrence M. *The Physics of Star Trek.* NY: Basic Books, 2001.

Leitch, Thomas. "Twelve Fallacies in Contemporary Adaptation Theory." *Criticism* 45.2 (Spring 2003): 149—71.

Lundeen, Jan and Wagner, Jon G. *Deep Space and Sacred Time:* Star Trek *in the American Mythos*. NY: Praeger, 1998.

McIntyre, Vonda N. *The Entropy Effect*. NY: Pocket Books, 1981.

Marx, Karl. *Capital Volume I.* NY: Modern Library, 1971.

Melville, Herman. *Moby-Dick; or, The Whale*. NY: Harper Brothers, 1851; Norwalk, CT: The Easton Press, 1977.

Nichols, Nichelle. *Beyond Uhura: Star Trek and Other Memories*. NY: Putnam, 1994.

Nimoy, Leonard. *I Am Not Spock.* Berkeley: Celestial Arts, 1976; reprinted NY: Buccaneer Books, 1997.

——. *I Am Spock*. NY: Hyperion, 1995.

Okrand, Marc. *The Klingon Dictionary.* NY: Pocket, 1992.

——. *The Klingon Way*. NY: Pocket, 1995.

——. *Klingon for the Galactic Traveler.* NY: Pocket, 1997.

Porter, Jennifer E., and McLaren, Darcee L., eds. *Star Trek and Sacred Ground: Explorations of Star Trek, Religion, and American Culture*. New York: State University of New York Press, 2000.

Proechel, Glen F. "Good News for the Klingon Race." *Bible Collector's World* October-December, 1994.

Raben, Richard and Hiyahuha Cohen. *Boldly Live as You've Never Lived Before: (Unauthorized and Unex-*

pected) *Life lessons from Star Trek*. NY: William Morrow, 1995.

Richards, Thomas. *The Meaning of Star Trek*. NY: Doubleday, 1997.

Rodriguez, John "Bones." *Captain Kirk's Guide to Women*. NY: Pocket, 2008.

Sakers, Don. "The Cold Solutions." *Analog Science Fiction/Science Fact*. July, 1991.

Schoen, Laurence and the Klingon Language Institute. *The Klingon Hamlet*. NY: Pocket, 2000.

Shelly, April. "'I Have Been, and Shall Ever Be, Your Friend': *Star Trek, The Deerslayer*, and the American Romance." *Journal of Popular Culture* 20.1 (1986): 89-104.

Satter, James. "The Hidden Homosexual: Reexamining *Star Trek*'s Sulu." *Science-Fiction Studies,* 33.2: 379-382.

Sky, Kathleen. *Vulcan!* NY: Bantam, 1975.

Takei, George. *To the Stars*. NY: Pocket, 1994.

Tetreault, Mary Ann. "The Trouble with *Star Trek*." *Minerva: The Journal of Women in the Military* 23.2 (1986): 119-129.

Whetmore, Edward. "A Female Captain's Enterprise: The Implication of *Star Trek*'s 'Turnabout Intruder.'" In *Future Females: A Critical Anthology*: 167-161. Marlene S. Barr, ed. Bowling Green, OH: Bowling Green State University Press, 1981.

Whitfield, Stephen E. and Roddenberry, Gene. *The Making of Star Trek*. NY: Ballantine, 1968.

Wilcox, Clyde. "To Boldly Return Where Others Have Gone Before: Cultural Change and the Old and New *Star Treks*." *Extrapolation* 33.1: 88-100.

INDEX

Episode Titles

Names and Terms

ABOUT THE AUTHOR

MICHAEL HEMMINGSON, an independent scholar, spends his time between Los Angeles and San Diego. His first feature film, *The Watermelon*, was released on DVD and Blu-Ray in 2009 from LightSong Films and Celebrity Video Distributors. He directed and narrated a short documentary, *Life in Zona Norte*, for Real Ideas Studio, which screened at the 2009 Cannes Film Festival. His critical studies include *The Dirty Realism Duo: Charles Bukowski and Raymond Carver* (2008); *William T. Vollmann* (2009); *The Role of Women in Raymond Carver's Short Fiction and Life* (2010); and *Gordon Lish and His Influence on 20th Century American Literature* (2010). He has also published some novels, short story collections, and edited a handful of anthologies, from *The Mammoth Book of Legal Thrillers* (2001) to *First Person Sociology* (2010).

www.ingramcontent.com/pod-product-compliance
Lightning Source LLC
Chambersburg PA
CBHW030937090426
42737CB00007B/463